THE
GREAT STEEL STRIKE
AND ITS LESSONS

A Da Capo Press Reprint Series

CIVIL LIBERTIES IN AMERICAN HISTORY

GENERAL EDITOR: LEONARD W. LEVY

Claremont Graduate School

THE
GREAT STEEL STRIKE
AND ITS LESSONS

By William Z. Foster

Introduction by John A. Fitch

DA CAPO PRESS · NEW YORK · 1971

A Da Capo Press Reprint Edition

This Da Capo Press edition of
The Great Steel Strike and Its Lessons
is an unabridged republication of the
first edition published in New York in 1920.

Library of Congress Catalog Card Number 70-139202

SBN 306-70079-4

Copyright, 1920, by B. W. Huebsch, Inc.

Published by Da Capo Press
A Division of Plenum Publishing Corporation
227 West 17th Street, New York, N.Y. 10011

THE GREAT STEEL STRIKE
AND ITS LESSONS

PENNSYLVANIA LAW AND ORDER

State Police driving peaceful citizens out of business places, Clairton, Pa.

THE
GREAT STEEL STRIKE
AND ITS LESSONS

BY

WILLIAM Z. FOSTER

INTRODUCTION BY
JOHN A. FITCH

NEW YORK
B. W. HUEBSCH, INC.
MCMXX

INTRODUCTION

Half a million men are employed in the steel industry of the United States. At a period in which eight hours is rapidly coming to be accepted as the standard length of the working day, the principal mills in this industry are operating on a 12-hour work schedule, and many of their workmen are employed seven days in every week. These half million men have, for the most part, no opportunity to discuss with their employers the conditions of their work. Not only are they denied the right of bargaining collectively over the terms of the labor contract, but if grievances arise in the course of their employment they have no right in any effective manner to take up the matter with their employer and secure an equitable adjustment.[1] The right even of petition has been at times denied and, because of the organized strength of the steel companies and the disorganized weakness of the employees, could be denied at any time.

The right of workers in this country to organize

[1] See for example Judge Gary's testimony before the Senate Committee investigating the steel strike — October 1, 1919, pp. 161–162, of committee hearings. He told of a strike which occurred because a grievance remained unadjusted after a committee of the workers had tried to take it up with the management. The president of the company involved was for crushing the strike without knowing what the grievance was or even of the existence of the committee.

and to bargain collectively is unquestioned. On every hand the workers are exercising this right in order to protect and advance their interests. In the steel mills not only is the right generally denied but the attempt to exercise it is punished by expulsion from the industry. Through a system of espionage that is thoroughgoing and effective the steel companies know which of their employees are attending union meetings, which of them are talking with organizers. It is their practice to discharge such men and thus they nip in the bud any ordinary movement toward organization.

Their power to prevent their employees from acting independently and in their own interest, extends even to the communities in which they live. In towns where the mayor's chair is occupied by company officials or their relatives — as was the case during the 1919 strike in Bethlehem, Duquesne, Clairton and elsewhere — orders may be issued denying to the workers the right to hold meetings for organizing purposes, or the police may be instructed to break them up. Elsewhere — as in Homestead, McKeesport, Monessen, Rankin and in Pittsburgh itself — the economic strength of the companies is so great as to secure the willing cooperation of officials or to compel owners of halls and vacant lots to refuse the use of their property for the holding of union meetings.

One who has not seen with his own eyes the evidences of steel company control in the towns where their plants are located will have difficulty in comprehending its scope and power. Social and religious organizations are profoundly affected by it.

In many a church during the recent strike, ministers and priests denounced the " agitators " and urged the workmen in their congregations to go back to the mills. Small business men accepted deputy sheriffs' commissions, put revolvers in their belts and talked loudly about the merits of a firing squad as a remedy for industrial unrest.

For twenty or more years in the mill towns along the Monongahela — since 1892 in Homestead — the working men have lived in an atmosphere of espionage and repression. The deadening influence of an overwhelming power, capable of crushing whatever does not bend to its will, has in these towns stifled individual initiative and robbed citizenship of its virility.

The story of the most extensive and most courageous fight yet made to break this power and to set free the half million men of the steel mills is told within the pages of this book by one who was himself a leader in the fight. It is a story that is worth the telling, for it has been told before only in fragmentary bits and without the authority that comes from the pen of one of the chief actors in the struggle.

Mr. Foster has performed a public service in setting down as he has the essential facts attendant upon the calling of the strike. The record of correspondence with Judge Gary and with President Wilson indicates clearly enough where responsibility for its occurrence lies. It answers the question also of who it was that flouted the President — the strike committee that refused to enter into a one sided truce, or Judge Gary, who would not accept Mr. Wilson's suggestion that he confer with a union committee, but who was willing to take advantage of the proposed truce to undermine and destroy the union.

This thoughtful history, remarkably dispassionate upon the whole, considering the fact that the author was not only an actor in the events he describes but the storm center of a countrywide campaign of slanderous falsehood, is an effective answer to those whose method of opposing the strike was to shout " Bolshevism " and " Revolution." Not thus are fomenters of revolution accustomed to write. It is this very quality which will make the book of great value both to the student and to the labor organizer. Never before has a leader in a great organizing campaign like the one preceding the steel strike sat down afterward to appraise so calmly the causes of defeat. Explanations of failure are common, usually in the form of " alibis." Mr. Foster has been willing to look the facts steadily in the face and his analysis of the causes of the loss of the strike — laying the responsibility for it at the doors of the unions themselves.— cannot fail to be helpful to every union leader, no matter what industry his union may represent. On the other hand his account of such a feat as the maintenance of a commissary adequate to meet the needs of the strikers at a cost of $1.40 per man is suggestive and encouraging to the highest degree. This achievement must stand as a monument to the integrity and practical ability of the men who conducted the strike.

It is with no purpose of underwriting every statement of fact or of making his own every theory advanced in the book that the writer expresses his confidence in it. It is because the book as a whole is so well done and because the essential message that it conveys is so true, that it is a pleasure to write these words of introduction. Other books have been written about the steel industry. Some have concerned themselves with metallurgy, others with the commercial aspects of steel manufacture, and still others with certain phases of the labor problem. This book is different from all the others. It sets forth as no other book has, and as no other writer could, the need of the workers in this great basic industry for organization, and the extreme difficulty of achieving this essential right. It shows also in the sanity, good temper, and straightforward speech of the author what sort of leadership it is that the steel companies have decreed their workers shall not have!

JOHN A. FITCH.

New York, June 4, 1920.

CONTENTS

                                                                    PAGE

INTRODUCTION v

CHAPTER
   I. THE PRESENT SITUATION 1

      The strike —" Victory " of the employers — Indus-
      trial democracy abroad, industrial serfdom at home
      — What the workers won — The outlook.

  II. A GENERATION OF DEFEAT 8

      The urge for mastery — Democratic resistance —
      The Homestead strike — The strikes of 1901 and
      1909 — The Steel Trust victorious.

 III. THE GIANT LABOR AWAKES 16

      A bleak prospect — Hope springs eternal — A
      golden chance — Disastrous delay — The new plan
      — A lost opportunity — The campaign begins —
      Gary fights back.

  IV. FLANK ATTACKS 28

      A sea of troubles — The policy of encirclement —
      Taking the outposts — Organizing methods — Fi-
      nancial systems — The question of morale — Johns-
      town.

   V. BREAKING INTO PITTSBURGH 50

      The flying squadron — Monessen — Donora — Mc-
      Keesport — Rankin — Braddock — Clairton — Home-
      stead — Duquesne — The results.

CHAPTER   PAGE

VI. STORM CLOUDS GATHER 68

   Relief demanded — The Amalgamated Association
   moves — A general movement — The conference
   committee — Gompers' letter unanswered — The
   strike vote — Gary defends steel autocracy — President Wilson acts in vain — The strike call.

VII. THE STORM BREAKS 96

   The Steel Trust Army — Corrupt officialdom —
   Clairton — McKeesport — The strike — showing by
   districts — A treasonable act — Gary gets his answer.

VIII. GARYISM RAMPANT 110

   The White Terror — Constitutional Rights denied
   — Unbreakable solidarity — Father Kazincy — The
   Cossacks — Scientific barbarity — Prostituted courts
   — Servants rewarded.

IX. EFFORTS AT SETTLEMENT 140

   The National Industrial Conference — The Senate
   committee — The red book — The Margolis case —
   The Interchurch World Movement.

X. THE COURSE OF THE STRIKE 162

   Pittsburgh district — The railroad men — Corrupt
   newspapers — Chicago district — Federal troops at
   Gary — Youngstown district — The Amalgamated
   Association — Cleveland — The Rod and Wire Mill
   strike — The Bethlehem plants — Buffalo and Lackawanna — Wheeling and Steubenville — Pueblo —
   Johnstown — Mob rule — The end of the strike.

XI. NATIONAL AND RACIAL ELEMENTS . . . 194

   A modern Babel — Americans as skilled workers —
   Foreigners as unskilled workers — Language difficulties — The Negro in the strike — The race problem.

CHAPTER   PAGE

XII. THE COMMISSARIAT — THE STRIKE COST   .   213

The Relief organization — Rations — System of distribution — Cost of Commissariat — Steel Strike Relief Fund — Cost of the strike to the workers, the
employers, the public, the Labor movement.

XIII. PAST MISTAKES AND FUTURE PROBLEMS .   . 234

Labor's lack of confidence — Inadequate efforts —
Need of alliance with miners and railroaders —
Radical leadership as a strike issue — Railroad
shopmen, Boston police, miners, railroad brotherhood strikes — Defection of Amalgamated Association.

XIV. IN CONCLUSION 255

The point of view — Are trade unions revolutionary? — Camouflage in social wars — Ruinous dual
unionism — Radicals should strengthen trade unions
— The English renaissance — Tom Mann's work.

ILLUSTRATIONS

Pennsylvania Law and Order . . . . . *Frontispiece*

FACING PAGE

National Committee Delegates 38

Strike Ballot 78

Cossacks in Action 122

Mrs. Fannie Sellins, Trade Union Organizer . . . 148

Steel Trust Newspaper Propaganda 188

John Fitzpatrick 216

A Group of Organizers 244

THE GREAT STEEL STRIKE
AND ITS LESSONS

THE
GREAT STEEL STRIKE
AND ITS LESSONS

I

THE PRESENT SITUATION

THE STRIKE —" VICTORY " OF THE EMPLOYERS —
INDUSTRIAL DEMOCRACY ABROAD, INDUSTRIAL
SERFDOM AT HOME — WHAT THE WORKERS
WON — THE OUTLOOK

THE great steel strike lasted three months and a
half. Begun on September 22, 1919, by 365,600
men quitting their places in the iron and steel mills
and blast furnaces in fifty cities of ten states, it
ended on January 8, 1920, when the organizations
affiliated in the National Committee for Organizing Iron and Steel Workers voted to permit the
100,000 or more men still on strike to return to work
upon the best terms they could secure.

The steel manufacturers " won " the strike. By
forcing an unconditional surrender, they drove their
men back to the old slavery. This they accomplished in their wonted and time-honored way by
carrying on a reign of terror that outraged every
just conception of civil and human rights. In this

[1]

unholy task they were aided by a crawling, subservient and lying press, which spewed forth its poison propaganda in their behalf; by selfish and indifferent local church movements, which had long since lost their Christian principles in an ignominious scramble for company favors; and by hordes of unscrupulous municipal, county, state and federal officials, whose eagerness to wear the steel collar was equalled only by their forgetfulness of their oaths of office. No suppression of free speech and free assembly, no wholesale clubbing, shooting and jailing of strikers and their families was too revolting for these Steel Trust [1] hangers-on to carry out with relish. With the notable exception of a few honorable and courageous individuals here and there among these hostile elements, it was an alignment of the steel companies, the state, the courts, the local churches and the press against the steel workers.

Upon the ending of the strike the steel workers got no direct concessions from their employers. Those who were able to evade the bitter blacklist were compelled to surrender their union cards and to return to work under conditions that are a shame and a disgrace. They were driven back to the in-

[1] Throughout this book the term "Steel Trust" is used to indicate the collectivity of the great steel companies. It is true that this is in contradiction to the common usage, which generally applies the term to the United States Steel Corporation alone, but it is in harmony with the facts. All the big steel companies act together upon all important matters confronting their industry. Beyond question they are organized more or less secretly into a trust. This book recognizes this situation, hence the broad use of the term "Steel Trust." It is important to remember this explanation. Where the writer has in mind any one company that company is named.

famous peonage system with its twelve hour day, a system which American steel workers, of all those in the world, alone have to endure. In England, France, Italy and Germany, the steel workers enjoy the right of a voice in the control of their industry; they regularly barter and bargain with their employers over the questions of hours, wages and working conditions; they also have the eight hour day. One must come to America, the land of freedom, to find steel workers still economically disfranchised and compelled to work twelve hours a day. In this country alone the human rights of the steel workers are crushed under foot by the triumphant property rights of their employers.

Who can uphold this indefensible position? Are not our deposits of coal and iron immeasurably greater, our mills more highly developed, our labor force more numerous and more skilled than those of any other country? Who then will venture to assert that American workingmen are not entitled to exercise all the rights and privileges enjoyed by European workingmen? If the steel workers of England, or France, or Italy, or Germany can practice collective bargaining, why not the steel workers of America? And why should the steel workers here have to work twelve hours daily when the eight hour day obtains abroad?

There are a hundred good reasons why the principles of collective bargaining and the shorter workday should prevail in the steel industry of America, and only one why they should not. This one reason is that the industry is hard and fast in the grip of absentee capitalists who take no part in production and whose sole function is to seize by hook or crook the product of the industry and consume it. These parasites, in their voracious quest of profits, know neither pity nor responsibility. Their reckless motto is " After us the deluge." They care less than naught for the rights and sufferings of the workers. Ignoring the inevitable weakening of patriotism of people living under miserable industrial conditions, they go their way, prostituting, strangling and dismembering our most cherished institutions. And the worst of it is that in the big strike an ignorant public, miseducated by employers' propaganda sheets masquerading under the guise of newspapers, applauded them in their ruthless course. Blindly this public, setting itself up as the great arbiter of what is democratic and American, condemned as bolshevistic and ruinous the demands of almost 400,000 steel workers for simple, fundamental reforms, without which hardly a pretense of freedom is possible, and lauded as sturdy Americanism the desperate autocracy of the Steel Trust. All its guns were turned against the strikers.

In this great struggle the mill owners may well claim the material victory; but with just as much right the workers can claim the moral victory. For the strike left in every aspiring breast a spark of hope which must burn on till it finally bursts into a flame of freedom-bringing revolt. For a generation steel workers had been hopeless. Their slavery had overwhelmed them. The trade-union movement seemed weak, distant and incapable. The rottenness of steel districts precluded all thought of relief through political channels. The employers

[4]

seemed omnipotent. But the strike has changed all this. Like a flash the unions appeared upon the scene. They flourished and expanded in spite of all opposition. Then boldly they went to a death grapple with the erstwhile unchallenged employers. It is true they did not win, but they put up a fight which has won the steel workers' hearts. Their earnest struggle and the loyal support, by money and food, which they gave the strikers, have forever laid at rest the employers' arguments that the unions are cowardly, grafting bodies organized merely to rob and betray the workers. Even the densest of the strikers could see that the loss of the strike was due to insufficient preparation; that only a fraction of the power of unionism had been developed and that with better organization better results would be secured. And the outcome is that the steel workers have won a precious belief in the power of concerted action through the unions. They have discovered the Achilles' heel of their would-be masters. They now see the way out of their slavery. This is their tremendous victory.

No less than the steel workers themselves, the whole trade-union movement won a great moral victory in the steel strike and the campaign that preceded it. This more than offsets the failure of the strike itself. The gain consists of a badly needed addition to the unions' thin store of self-confidence. To trade-union organizers the steel industry had long symbolized the impossible. Wave after wave of organizing effort they had sent against it; but their work had been as ineffectual as a summer sea lapping the base of Gibraltar. Pessimism regarding its conquest for trade unionism was abysmal. But now all this is changed. The impossible has been accomplished. The steel workers were organized in the face of all that the steel companies could do to prevent it. Thus a whole new vista of possibilities unfolds before the unions. Not only does the reorganization of the steel industry seem strictly feasible, but the whole conception that many of the basic industries are immune to trade unionism turns out to be an illusion. If the steel industry could be organized, so can any other in the country; for the worst of them presents hardly a fraction of the difficulties squarely vanquished in the steel industry. The mouth has been shut forever of that insufferable pest of the labor movement, the large body of ignorant, incompetent, short-sighted, visionless union men whose eternal song, when some important organizing project is afoot, is " It can't be done." After this experience in the steel industry the problem of unionizing any industry resolves itself simply into selecting a capable organizer and giving him sufficient money and men to do the job.

The ending of the strike by no means indicates the abandonment of the steel workers' battle for their rights. For a while, perhaps, their advance may be checked, while they are recovering from the effects of their great struggle. But it will not be long before they have another big movement under way. They feel but little defeated by the loss of the strike, and the trade unions as a whole feel even less so. Both have gained wonderful confidence in themselves and in each other during the fight. The unions will not desert the field and leave the workers

[6]

a prey to the demoralizing propaganda of the employers, customary after lost strikes. On the contrary they are keeping a large crew of organizers at work in an educational campaign, devised to maintain and develop the confidence the steel workers have in themselves and the unions. Then, when the opportune time comes, which will be but shortly, the next big drive will be on. Mr. Gary and his associates may attempt to forestall the inevitable by the granting of fake eight hour days, paper increases in wages and hand-picked company unions, but it is safe to say that the steel workers will go on building up stronger and more aggressive combinations among themselves and with allied trades until they finally achieve industrial freedom. So long as any men undertake to oppress the steel workers and to squeeze returns from the industry without rendering adequate service therefor, just that long must these men expect to be confronted by a progressively more militant and rebellious working force. The great steel strike of 1919 will seem only a preliminary skirmish when compared with the tremendous battles that are bound to come unless the enslaved steel workers are set free.

II

A GENERATION OF DEFEAT [1]

THE URGE FOR MASTERY — DEMOCRATIC RESIST-
ANCE — THE HOMESTEAD STRIKE — THE STRIKES
OF 1901 AND 1909 — THE STEEL TRUST VIC-
TORIOUS

THE recent upheaval in the steel industry was but
one link in a long chain of struggles, the latest battle
in an industrial war for freedom which has raged
almost since the inception of the industry.

The steel manufacturers have always aggressively
applied the ordinary, although unacknowledged,
American business principles that our industries
exist primarily to create huge profits for the for-
tunate few who own them, and that if they have
any other utility it is a matter of secondary importance. The interests of society in the steel business
they scoff at. And as for their own employees, they
have never considered them better than so much
necessary human machinery, to be bought in the
market at the lowest possible price and otherwise
handled in a thoroughly irresponsible manner.
They clearly understand that if they are to carry out
their policy of raw exploitation, the prime essential

[1] Students desiring a full account of the early struggles of the
steel unions are advised to read Mr. John A. Fitch's splendid
book, " The Steel Workers."

[8]

is that they keep their employees unorganized. Then, without let or hindrance, wages may be kept low, the work day made longer, speeding systems introduced, safety devices neglected, and the human side of the industry generally robbed and repressed in favor of its profit side; whereas, if the unions were allowed to come in, it would mean that every policy in the industry would first have to be considered and judged with regard to its effects upon the men actually making steel and iron. It would mean that humanity must be emphasized at the expense of misearned dividends. But this would never do. The mill owners are interested in profits, not in humanity. Hence, if they can prevent it, they will have no unions. Since the pioneer days of steel making their policy has tended powerfully on the one hand towards elevating the employers into a small group of enormously wealthy, idle, industrial autocrats, and on the other towards depressing the workers into a huge army of ignorant, poverty-stricken, industrial serfs. The calamity of it is that this policy has worked out so well.

Against this will-to-power of their employers the steel workers have fought long and valiantly. In the early days of the industry, when the combinations of capital were weak, the working force skilled, English-speaking and independent, the latter easily defended themselves and made substantial progress toward their own inevitable, even if unrecognized goal of industrial freedom; but in later years, with the growth of the gigantic United States Steel Corporation, the displacement of skilled labor by automatic machinery and the introduction of multitudes

[9]

of illiterate immigrants into the industry, their fight for their rights became a desperate and almost hopeless struggle. For the past thirty years they have suffered an unbroken series of defeats. Their one-time growing freedom has been crushed.

At first the fight was easy, and by the later '80's, grace to the activities of many unions, notable among which were the old Sons of Vulcan, the Knights of Labor and the Amalgamated Association of Iron, Steel and Tin Workers, considerable organization existed among the men employed in the iron and steel mills throughout the country. The Amalgamated Association, the dominating body, enjoyed great prestige in the labor movement generally. It consisted almost entirely of highly skilled men and paid little or no attention to the unskilled workers. In the heyday of its strength, in 1891, it numbered about 24,000 members. Its stronghold was in the Pittsburgh district. Its citadel was Homestead. During the period of its greatest activity some measure of democracy prevailed in the industry, and prospects seemed bright for its extension.

But about that time Andrew Carnegie, grown rich and powerful, began to chafe uneasily under the restrictions placed upon his rapacity by his organized employees. He wanted a free hand and determined to get it. As the first step towards enshackling his workers he brought into his company that inveterate enemy of democracy in all its forms, Henry C. Frick. Then the two, Carnegie and Frick, neither of whom gave his workers as much consideration as the Southern slave holder gave his bondmen — for chattel slaves were at least assured sufficient food, warm

clothes, a habitable home and medical attendance —
began to war upon the union. They started the
trouble in Homestead, where the big mills of the
Carnegie Company are located. In 1889 they insisted that the men accept heavy reductions in wages,
write their agreements to expire in the unfavorable
winter season instead of in summer, and give up their
union. The men refused, and after a short strike,
got a favorable settlement. But Carnegie and
Frick were not to be lightly turned from their purpose. When the contract in force expired, they renewed their old demands, and thus precipitated the
great Homestead strike.

This famous strike attracted world-wide attention, and well it might, for it marked a turning point
in the industrial history of America. It began on
June 23, 1892, and lasted until November 20 of the
same year. Characterized by extreme bitterness
and violence, it resulted in complete defeat for the
men, not only in Homestead, but also in several
other big mills in Pittsburgh and adjoining towns
where the steel workers had struck in support of
their besieged brothers in Homestead. This unsuccessful strike eliminated organized labor from the
mills of the big Carnegie Company. It also dealt
the Amalgamated Association of Iron, Steel and Tin
Workers a blow from which it has not yet recovered.
It ended the period of trade-union expansion in the
steel industry and began an era of unrestricted labor
control by the employers. At Homestead Carnegie
and Frick stuck a knife deep into the vitals of the
young democracy of the steel workers.

Recuperating somewhat from the staggering defeat at Homestead, the Amalgamated Association managed to retain a firm hold in the industry for a few years longer. Its next big setback, in 1901, was caused by the organization of the United States Steel Corporation. Foreseeing war from this monster combination dominated by the hostile Carnegie interests, the union, presided over at that time by Theodore J. Shaffer, decided to take time by the forelock and negotiate an agreement that would extend its scope and give it a chance to live. But the plan failed; the anti-union tendencies of the employers were too strong, and a strike resulted. At first the only companies affected were the American Tin Plate Company, the American Sheet Steel Company and the American Steel Hoop Company. Finally, however, all the organized men in all the mills of the United States Steel Corporation were called out, but to no avail; after a few weeks' struggle the strike was utterly lost.

The failure of the 1901 strike broke the backbone of the Amalgamated Association. Still, with characteristic trade-union tenacity, it lingered along in a few of the Trust plants in the sheet and tin section of the industry. Its business relations with the companies at this stage of its decline, according to the testimony of its present President, M. F. Tighe, before the Senate Committee investigating the 1919 strike, consisted of " giving way to every request that was made by the companies when they insisted upon it." But even this humble and pliant attitude of the once powerful Amalgamated Association was intolerable to the haughty steel kings. They could not brook even the most shadowy opposition to their industrial absolutism. Accordingly, early in the summer of 1909, they served notice upon the union men to accept a reduction in wages and give up their union. It was practically the same ultimatum delivered by Carnegie and Frick to the Homestead men twenty years before. With a last desperate rally the union met this latest attack upon its life. The ensuing strike lasted fourteen months. It was bitterly fought, but it went the way of all strikes in the steel industry since 1892. It was lost; and in consequence every trace of unionism was wiped out of the mills not only of the United States Steel Corporation, but of the big independent companies as well.

Although the union was not finally crushed in the mills until the strike of 1909, the steel mill owners were for many years previous to that time in almost undisputed control of the situation. During a generation, practically, they have worked their will unhampered; and the results of their policy of unlimited exploitation are all too apparent. For themselves they have taken untold millions of wealth from the industry; for the workers they have left barely enough to eke out an existence in the miserable, degraded steel towns.

At the outbreak of the World war the steel workers generally, with the exception of the laborers, who had secured a cent or two advance per hour, were making less wages than before the Homestead strike. The constant increase in the cost of living in the intervening years had still further depressed their standards of life. Not a shred of benefit had they received from the tremendously

[13]

increased output of the industry. While the employers lived in gorgeous palaces, the workers found themselves, for the most part, crowded like cattle into the filthy hovels that ordinarily constitute the greater part of the steel towns. Tuberculosis ran riot among them; infant mortality was far above normal. Though several increases in wages were granted after the war began, these have been offset by the terrific rise in the cost of living. If the war has brought any betterment in the living conditions of the steel workers, it cannot be seen with the naked eye.

The twelve hour day prevails for half of the men. One-fourth work seven days a week, with a twenty-four hour shift every two weeks. Their lives are one constant round of toil. They have no family life, no opportunity for education or even for recreation; for their few hours of liberty are spoiled by the ever-present fatigue. Furthermore, working conditions in the mills are bad. The men are speeded up to such a degree that only the youngest and strongest can stand it. At forty the average steel worker is played out. The work, in itself extremely dangerous, is made still more so by the employers' failure to adopt the necessary safety devices. Many a man has gone to his death through the wanton neglect of the companies to provide safeguarding appliances that they would have been compelled to install were the unions still in the plants.[1]

[1] The practice of the different steel companies varies with respect to safety devices. Some of them are still in the dark ages that all were in a few years ago, with reckless disregard of human life. Others have made some progress. Of these the U. S. Steel Corporation is undoubtedly in the lead, for it has installed many safety appliances and has safety committees actively at work. At

Not a trace of industrial justice remains. The treatment of the men depends altogether upon the arbitrary wills of the foremen and superintendents. A man may give faithful service in a plant for thirty years and then be discharged offhand, as many are, for some insignificant cause. He has no one to appeal to. His fellow workers, living in constant terror of discharge and the blacklist, dare not even listen to him, much less defend his cause. He must bow to the inevitable, even though it means industrial ruin for him and his family.

Such deplorable conditions result naturally from a lack of unionism. It is expecting too much of human nature at this stage of its development to count on employers treating their employees fairly without some form of compulsion. Even in highly organized industries the unions have to be constantly on guard to resist the never-ending encroachments of their employers, manifested at every conceivable point of attack. For the workers, indeed, eternal vigilance is the price of liberty. Hence nothing but degradation for them and autocracy for their employers may be looked for in industries where they are systematically kept unorganized and thus incapable of defending their rights, as is the case in the steel industry. This system of industrial serfdom has served the steel barons well for a generation. But it is one the steel workers will never accept. Regardless of the cost they will rebel against it at every opportunity till they finally destroy it.

best, however, steel making is an exceedingly dangerous industry and the risk is intensified by the great heat of the mills and the long hours of work — the twelve hour day and the seven day week — which lead inevitably to exhaustion.

III

THE GIANT LABOR AWAKES

A BLEAK PROSPECT — HOPE SPRINGS ETERNAL —
A GOLDEN CHANCE — DISASTROUS DELAY — THE
NEW PLAN — A LOST OPPORTUNITY — THE CAM-
PAIGN BEGINS — GARY FIGHTS BACK

FROM just previous to, until some time after the
beginning of the world war the situation in the steel
industry, from a trade-union point of view, was truly
discouraging. It seemed impossible for the workers
to accomplish anything by organized effort. The
big steel companies, by driving the Amalgamated Association of Iron, Steel and Tin Workers from the
mills, had built up a terrific reputation as union
crushers. This was greatly enhanced by their complete defeat of Labor in the memorable strikes of the
structural iron workers, the lake sailors, the iron
miners, and the steel workers at McKees Rocks in
1909, Bethlehem in 1910 and Youngstown in
1915–16. It was still further enhanced by their
blocking every attempt of the individual trades to re-
establish themselves, and by the failure of the A. F.
of L. steel campaign, inaugurated by the convention
of 1909, to achieve even the slightest tangible results. The endless round of defeat had reduced
almost to zero the trade unions' confidence in their

ability to cope with the militant and rapacious steel manufacturers.

But as the war wore on and the United States joined the general slaughter, the situation changed rapidly in favor of the unions. The demand for soldiers and munitions had made labor scarce; the Federal administration was friendly; the right to organize was freely conceded by the government and even insisted upon; the steel industry was the master-clock of the whole war program and had to be kept in operation at all costs; the workers were taking new heart and making demands — already they had engaged in big strike movements in the mills in Pittsburgh (Jones and Laughlin Company), Bethlehem and Birmingham (U. S. Steel). The gods were indeed fighting on the side of Labor. It was an opportunity to organize the industry such as might never again occur. That the trade union movement did not embrace it sooner was a calamity.

The writer was one of those who perceived the unparalleled opportunity. But being at that time Secretary-Treasurer of the committee organizing the packing industry I was unable to do anything substantial in the steel situation until the handing down of Judge Alschuler's decision giving the packing house workers the eight hour day and other vital concessions enabled me to slacken my efforts in that important movement. Immediately thereafter, on April 7, 1918, I presented a resolution to the Chicago Federation of Labor requesting the executive officers of the American Federation of Labor to call a general labor conference and to inaugurate thereat a national campaign to organize the steel workers.

[17]

The resolution was endorsed by twelve local unions in the steel industry. It was adopted unanimously and forwarded to the A. F. of L. The latter took the matter up with the rapidly reviving Amalgamated Association, and the affair was slowly winding along to an eventual conference, with a loss of much precious time, when the resolution was re-submitted to the Chicago Federation of Labor, re-adopted and sent to the St. Paul convention of the A. F. of L., June 10–20, 1918. It follows:

RESOLUTION #29

Whereas, the organization of the vast armies of wage-earners employed in the steel industries is vitally necessary to the further spread of industrial democracy in America, and

Whereas, Organized Labor can accomplish this great task only by putting forth a tremendous effort; therefore, be it

Resolved, that the executive officers of the A. F. of L. stand instructed to call a conference during this convention of delegates of all international unions whose interests are involved in the steel industries, and of all the State Federations and City Central bodies in the steel districts, for the purpose of uniting all these organizations into one mighty drive to organize the steel plants of America.

The resolution was adopted by unanimous vote. Accordingly, a number of conferences were held during the convention, at which the proposed campaign was discussed and endorsed. The outcome was that provisions were made to have President Gompers call another conference, in Chicago thirty days later, of responsible union officials who would come prepared to act in the name of their international unions. This involved further waste of probably the most precious time for organizing work that Labor will ever have.

From past events in the steel industry it was evident that in the proposed campaign radical departures would have to be made from the ordinary organizing tactics. Without question the steel workers' unions have always lacked efficiency in their organizing departments. This was a cardinal failing of the Amalgamated Association and it contributed as much, if not more than anything else to its downfall. If, when in its prime, this organization had shown sufficient organizing activity in the non-union mills, and especially by taking in the unskilled, it would have so intrenched itself that Carnegie and his henchman, Frick, never could have dislodged it. But, unfortunately, it undertook too much of its organization work at the conference table and not enough at the mill gates. Consequently, more than once it found itself in deadly quarrels with the employers over the unionization of certain mills, when a live organizer working among the non-union men involved would have solved the problem in a few weeks.

Nor had the other unions claiming jurisdiction over men employed in the steel industry developed an organizing policy equal to the occasion. Their system of nibbling away, one craft at a time in individual mills, was entirely out of place. Possibly effective in some industries, it was worse than useless in the steel mills. Its unvarying failure served only to strengthen the mill owners and to further

[19]

discourage the mill workers and Organized Labor. It is pure folly to organize one trade in one mill, or all trades in one mill, or even all trades in all the mills in one locality, when, at any time it sees fit to do so, the Steel Trust can defeat the movement by merely shutting down its mills in the affected district and transferring its work elsewhere, as it has done time and again. It was plain, therefore, that the proposed campaign would have to affect all the steel mills simultaneously. It would have to be national in scope and encompass every worker in every mill, in every steel district in the United States.

The intention was to use the system so strikingly successful in the organization of the packing industry. The committee charged with organizing that industry, when it assembled, a year before, to begin the work, found three possible methods of procedure confronting it, each with its advocates present. It could go along on the old, discredited craft policy of each trade for itself and the devil take the hindmost; it might attempt to form an industrial union; or it could apply the principle of federating the trades, then making great headway on the railroads. The latter system was the one chosen as the best fitted to get results at this stage in the development of the unions and the packing industry. And the outcome proved the wisdom of the decision. In the steel campaign the unions were to be similarly linked together in an offensive and defensive alliance.

But all this relates merely to the shell of the plan behind Resolution No. 29. Its breath of life was in its strategy; in the way the organization work was to be prosecuted. The best plans are

[20]

worthless unless properly executed. The idea was to make a hurricane drive simultaneously in all the steel centers that would catch the workers' imagination and sweep them into the unions *en masse* despite all opposition, and thus to put Mr. Gary and his associates into such a predicament that they would have to grant the just demands of their men. It was intended that after the Chicago conference a dozen or more general organizers should be dispatched immediately to the most important steel centers, to bring to the steel workers the first word of the big drive being made in their behalf, and to organize local committees to handle the detail work of organization. In the meantime the co-operating international unions were to recruit numbers of organizers and to send them to join the forces already being developed everywhere by the general organizers. They should also assemble and pay in as quickly as possible their respective portions of the fund of at least $250,000 to be provided for the work. The essence of the plan was quick, energetic action.

At the end of three or four weeks, when the organizing forces were in good shape and the workers in the mills acquainted with what was afoot, the campaign would be opened with a rush. Great mass meetings, built up by extensive advertising, would be held everywhere at the same time throughout the steel industry. These were calculated to arouse hope and enthusiasm among the workers and to bring thousands of them into the unions, regardless of any steps the mill owners might take to prevent it. After two or three meetings in each place, the heavy stream of men pouring into the unions would be turned into a decisive flood by the election of committees to formulate the grievances of the men and present these to the employers. The war was on; the continued operation of the steel industry was imperative; a strike was therefore out of the question; the steel manufacturers would have been compelled to yield to their workers, either directly or through the instrumentality of the Government. The trade unions would have been re-established in the steel industry, and along with them fair dealing and the beginnings of industrial democracy.

The plan was not only a bold one, but also under the circumstances the logical and practical one. The course of events proved its feasibility. The contention that it involved taking unfair advantage of the steel manufacturers may be dismissed as inconsequential. These gentlemen in their dealings with those who stand in their way do not even know the meaning of the word fairness. Their workers they shoot and starve into submission; their competitors they industrially strangle without ceremony; the public and the Government they exploit without stint or limit. The year before the campaign began, 1917, when the country was straining every nerve to develop and conserve its resources, the United States Steel Corporation alone, not to mention the many independents, after paying federal taxes and leaving out of account the vast sums that disappeared in the obscure and mysterious company funds, unblushingly pocketed the fabulous profit of $253,608,200.

It now remained to be seen how far the unions

would sustain such a general and energetic campaign. The fateful conference met in the New Morrison Hotel, Chicago, August 1–2, 1918. Samuel Gompers presided over its sessions. Representatives of fifteen international unions were present. These men showed their progressive spirit by meeting many difficult issues squarely with the proper solutions. They realized fully the need of co-operation along industrial lines, from the men who dig the coal and iron ore to those who switch the finished products onto the main lines of the railroads. Plainly no trade felt able to cope single-handed with the Steel Trust; and joint action was decided upon almost without discussion. Likewise the conference saw the folly of trying to organize the steel industry with each of the score of unions demanding a different initiation fee. Therefore, after much stretching of constitutions, the international unions, with the exception of the Bricklayers, Molders and Patternmakers (who charged respectively $7.25, $5.00 and $5.00), agreed to a uniform initiation fee of three dollars, one dollar of which was to be used for defraying expenses of the national organization work.

At the same meeting the National Committee for Organizing Iron and Steel Workers was formed. It was made to consist of one representative from each of the co-operating international unions. Its given function was to superintend the work of organization. Its chairman had to be a representative of the A. F. of L. Mr. Gompers volunteered to fill this position; the writer was elected Secretary-Treasurer. Including later additions, the constituent unions were as follows:

International Brotherhood of Blacksmiths, Drop-Forgers and Helpers

Brotherhood of Boilermakers and Iron Ship Builders and Helpers of America

United Brick and Clay Workers

Bricklayers', Masons' and Plasterers' International Union of America

International Association of Bridge, Structural and Ornamental Iron Workers

Coopers' International Union of North America

International Brotherhood of Electrical Workers

International Brotherhood of Foundry Employees

International Hod Carriers', Building, and Common Laborers' Union of America

Amalgamated Association of Iron, Steel and Tin Workers

International Association of Machinists

International Union of Mine, Mill and Smelter Workers

United Mine Workers of America

International Molders' Union of North America

Patternmakers' League of North America

United Association of Plumbers and Steam Fitters

Quarry Workers' International Union of North America

Brotherhood Railway Carmen of America

International Seamen's Union of America

Amalgamated Sheet Metal Workers' International Alliance

International Brotherhood of Stationary Firemen and Oilers

International Union of Steam and Operating Engineers

International Brotherhood of Steamshovel and Dredgemen

Switchmen's Union of North America.

This group of unions, lined up to do battle with the Steel Trust, represents the largest body of workers ever engaged in a joint movement in any country. Their members number approximately 2,000,000, and comprise about one-half of the entire American Federation of Labor.

So far, so good. The conference had removed the barriers in the way of the campaign. But when it came to providing the large sums of money and the numerous crews of organizers that were immediately and imperatively needed to insure success, it failed dismally. The internationals assessed themselves only $100 apiece; they furnished only a corporal's guard of organizers to go ahead with the work; and future reinforcements looked remote.

This was a facer. The original plan of a dashing offensive went to smash instanter, and with it, likewise, the opportunity to organize the steel industry. The slender resources in hand at once made necessary a complete change of strategy. To undertake a national movement was out of the question. The work had to be confined to the Chicago district. This was admittedly going according to wrong principles. The steel industry is national in scope and should be handled as such. To operate in one district alone would expose that district to attacks, waste invaluable time and give the employers a chance to adopt counter measures against the whole campaign. It meant playing squarely into Mr. Gary's hands. But there was no other way out of the difficulty.

The writer had hoped that the favorable industrial situation and the organization of the packing industry, which had long been considered hopeless, would have heartened the trade-union movement sufficiently for it to attack the steel problem with the required vigor and confidence. But such was not the case. The tradition of defeat in the steel industry was too strong,— thirty years of failure were not so easily forgotten. Lack of faith in themselves prevented the unions from pouring their resources into the campaign in its early, critical days. The work in the Chicago district was undertaken, nevertheless, with a determination to win the hearty support of Labor by giving an actual demonstration of the organizability of the steel workers.

During the first week of September the drive for members was opened in the Chicago district. Monster meetings were held in South Chicago, Gary, Indiana Harbor and Joliet — all the points that the few organizers could cover. The inevitable happened; eager for a chance to right their wrongs, the steel workers stormed into the unions. In Gary 749 joined at the first meeting, Joliet enrolled 500, and other places did almost as well. It was a stampede — exactly what was counted upon by the movers of Resolution #29. And it could just as well have been on a national scale, had the international unions possessed sufficient self-confidence and given enough men and money to put the original plan into execution. In a few weeks the unions would have been everywhere firmly intrenched; and in a few more the entire steel industry would have been captured for trade unionism and justice.

But now the folly of a one-district movement made itself evident. Up to this time the steel barons, like many union leaders, apparently had viewed the campaign with a skeptical, " It can't be done " air. But events in Gary and elsewhere quickly dissipated their optimism. The movement was clearly dangerous and required heroic treatment. The employers, therefore, applying Mr. Gary's famous " Give them an extra cup of rice " policy, ordered the basic eight hour day to go into effect on the first of October. This meant that the steel workers were to get thereafter time and one half after eight hours, instead of straight time. It amounted to an increase of two hours pay per day but the actual working hours were not changed. It was a counter stroke which the national movement had been designed to forestall.

Although this concession really spelled a great moral victory for the unions its practical effect was bad. Just a few months before the United States Steel Corporation had publicly announced that, come what might, there would be no basic eight hour day in the steel industry. Its sudden adoption, almost over night, therefore, was a testimonial to the power of the unions. But this the steel workers as a whole could not realize. In the Chicago district, where the campaign was on, they understood and gave the unions credit for the winning; but in other districts, where nothing had been done, naturally they believed it a gift from the companies. Had the work been going on everywhere when Mr. Gary attempted this move, the workers would have understood his motives and joined the unions *en masse,*— the unions would have won hands down. But with operations confined to one district he was able to steal the credit from the unions, partially satisfy his men, and strip the campaign of one of its principal issues. No doubt he thought he had dealt it a mortal blow.

IV

FLANK ATTACKS

A SEA OF TROUBLES — THE POLICY OF ENCIRCLE-
MENT — TAKING THE OUTPOSTS — ORGANIZING
METHODS — FINANCIAL SYSTEMS — THE QUES-
TION OF MORALE — JOHNSTOWN

PITTSBURGH is the heart of America's steel industry.
Its pre-eminence derives from its splendid location
for steel making.   It is situated at the point where
the Allegheny and Monongahela rivers join their
murky waters to form the Ohio, this providing excellent water transportation.   Immense deposits of
coal surround it; the Great Lakes, the gateway to
Minnesota's iron ore, are in easy reach; highly developed railway facilities make the best markets
convenient.   In the city itself there are only a few
of the larger steel mills; but at short distances along
the banks of its three rivers, are many big steel
producing centers, including Homestead, Braddock,
Rankin, McKeesport, McKees Rocks, Duquesne,
Clairton, Woodlawn, Donora, Midland, Vandergrift, Brackenridge, New Kensington, etc.   Within
a radius of seventy-five miles lie Johnstown, Youngstown, Butler, Farrell, Sharon, New Castle, Wheeling, Mingo, Steubenville, Bellaire, Wierton and

[28]

various other important steel towns. The district contains from seventy to eighty per cent. of the country's steel industry. The whole territory is an amazing and bewildering network of gigantic steel mills, blast furnaces and fabricating shops.

It was into this industrial labyrinth, the den of the Steel Trust, that the National Committee for Organizing Iron and Steel Workers moved its office on October 1, 1918, preparatory to beginning its work. Success in the Chicago district had made it imperative to overcome the original tactical blunder by extending the campaign, just as quickly as possible, to a national scope.

The outlook was most unpromising. Even under the best of circumstances the task of getting the enormous army of steel workers to thinking and acting together in terms of trade unionism would be tremendous. But the disastrous mistake of not starting the campaign soon enough and with the proper vigor multiplied the difficulties. Unfavorable winter weather was approaching. This was complicated by the influenza epidemic, which for several weeks suspended all public gatherings. Then came the end of the war. The workers had also just been given the basic eight hour day. All these things tended to still them somewhat and to weaken their interest in organization. What was left of this interest was almost entirely wiped out when the mills, dependent as they were on war work, began to slacken production. The workers became obsessed with a fear of hard times, a timidity which was intensified by the steel companies' discharging every one suspected of union affiliations or sympathies. And to cap the climax, the resources of the National Committee were still pitifully inadequate to the great task confronting it.

But worst of all, the steel companies were now on the *qui vive*. The original plan had been conceived to take them by surprise, on the supposition that their supreme contempt for Labor and their conceit in their own power would blind them to the real force and extent of the movement until it was too late to take effective counteraction. And it would surely have worked out this way, had the program been followed. But now the advantage of surprise, vital in all wars, industrial or military, was lost to the unions. Wide awake and alarmed, the Steel Trust was prepared to fight to the last ditch.

Things looked desperate. But there was no other course than to go ahead regardless of obstacles. The word failure was eliminated from the vocabulary of the National Committee. Preparations were made to begin operations in the towns close to Pittsburgh. But the Steel Trust was vigilant. It no longer placed any reliance upon its usual methods — its welfare, old age pension, employees' stockholding, wholesale discharge, or " extra cup of rice " policies — to hold its men in line, when a good fighting chance to win their rights presented itself to them. It had gained a wholesome respect for the movement and was taking no chances. It would cut off all communication between the organizers and the men. Consequently, its lackey-like mayors and burgesses in the threatened towns immediately held a meeting and decided that there would be no assemblages of steel workers in the Monongahela valley.   In some places these officials, who for the most part are steel company employees, had the pliable local councils hurriedly adopt ordinances making it unlawful to hold public meetings without securing sanction; in other places they adopted the equally effective method of simply notifying the landlords that if they dared rent their halls to the American Federation of Labor they would have their " Sunday Club " privileges stopped.   In both cases the effect was the same — no meetings could be held. In the immediate Pittsburgh district there had been little enough free speech and free assembly for the trade unions before.   Now it was abolished altogether.

At this time the world war was still on; our soldiers were fighting in Europe to " make the world safe for democracy "; President Wilson was idealistically declaiming about " the new freedom "; while right here in our own country the trade unions, with 500,000 men in the service, were not even allowed to hold public meetings.   It was a worse condition than kaiserism itself had ever set up.   This is said advisedly, for the German workers were at least permitted to meet when and where they pleased. The worst they had to contend with was a policeman on their platform, who would jot down " seditious " remarks and require the offenders to report next day to the police.   I remember with what scorn I watched this system in Germany years ago, and how proud I felt to be an American.   I was so sure that freedom of speech and assembly were fundamental institutions with us and that we would never tolerate such imposition.   But now I have changed my

[31]

mind.   In Pennsylvania, not to speak of other states, the workers enjoy few or no more rights than prevailed under the czars.   They cannot hold meetings at all.   So far are they below the status of pre-war Germans in this respect that the comparative freedom of the latter seems almost like an unattainable ideal.   And this deprival of rights is done in the name of law and patriotism.

In the face of such suppression of constitutional rights and in the face of all the other staggering difficulties it was clearly impossible for our scanty forces to capture Pittsburgh for unionism by a frontal attack.   Therefore a system of flank attacks was decided upon.   This resolved itself into a plan literally to surround the immediate Pittsburgh district with organized posts before attacking it.   The outlying steel districts that dot the counties and states around Pittsburgh like minor forts about a great stronghold, were first to be won.   Then the unions, with the added strength, were to make a big drive on the citadel.

It was a far-fetched program when compared with the original; but circumstances compelled it.   An important consideration in its execution was that it must not seem that the unions were abandoning Pittsburgh.   That was the center of the battle line; the unions had attacked there, and now they must at least pretend to hold their ground until they were able to begin the real attack.   The morale of the organizing force and the steel workers demanded this.   So, all winter long mass meetings were held in the Pittsburgh Labor Temple and hundreds of thousands of leaflets were distributed in the neighboring mills to prepare the ground for unionization in the spring. Besides, a lot of noise was made over the suppression of free speech and free assemblage. Protest meetings were held, committees appointed, investigations set afoot, politicians visited, and much other more or less useless, although spectacular, running around engaged in. These activities did not cost much, and they camouflaged well the union program.

But the actual fight was elsewhere. During the next several months the National Committee, with gradually increasing resources, set up substantial organizations in steel towns all over the country except close in to Pittsburgh, including Youngstown, East Youngstown, Warren, Niles, Canton, Struthers, Hubbard, Massillon, Alliance, New Philadelphia, Sharon, Farrell, New Castle, Butler, Ellwood City, New Kensington, Leechburg, Apollo, Vandergrift, Brackenridge, Johnstown, Coatesville, Wheeling, Benwood, Bellaire, Steubenville, Mingo, Cleveland, Buffalo, Lackawanna, Pueblo, Birmingham, etc. Operations in the Chicago district were intensified and extended to take in Milwaukee, Kenosha, Waukegan, De Kalb, Peoria, Pullman, Hammond, East Chicago, etc., while in Bethlehem the National Committee amplified the work started a year before by the Machinists and Electrical Workers.

Much of the success in these localities was due to the thoroughly systematic way in which the organizing work was carried on. This merits a brief description. There were two classes of organizers in the campaign, the floating and the stationary. Outside of a few traveling foreign speakers, the float-

[33]

ing organizers were those sent in by the various international unions. They usually went about from point to point attending to their respective sections of the newly formed local unions, and giving such assistance to the general campaign as their other duties permitted. The stationary organizers consisted of A. F. of L. men, representatives of the United Mine Workers, and men hired directly by the National Committee. They acted as local organizing secretaries, and were the backbone of the working force. The floating organizers were controlled mostly by their international unions; the stationary organizers worked wholly under the direction of the National Committee.

Everywhere the organizing system used was the same. The local secretary was in full charge. He had an office, which served as general headquarters. He circulated the National Committee's weekly bulletin, consisting of a short, trenchant trade-union argument in four languages. He built up the mass meetings, and controlled all applications for membership. At these mass meetings and in the offices all trades were signed up indiscriminately upon a uniform blank. But there was no " one big union " formed. The signed applications were merely stacked away until there was a considerable number. Then the representatives of all the trades were assembled and the applications distributed among them. Later these men set up their respective unions. Finally, the new unions were drawn up locally into informal central bodies, known as Iron and Steel Workers' councils. These were invaluable as they knit the movement together and strengthened the weaker unions. They also inculcated the indispensable conception of solidarity along industrial lines and prevented irresponsible strike action by over-zealous single trades.

A highly important feature was the financial system. The handling of the funds is always a danger point in all working class movements. More than one strike and organizing campaign has been wrecked by loose money methods. The National Committee spared no pains to avoid this menace. The problem was an immense one, for there were from 100 to 125 organizers (which was what the crew finally amounted to) signing up steel workers by the thousands all over the country; but it was solved by the strict application of a few business principles. In the first place the local secretaries were definitely recognized as the men in charge and placed under heavy bonds. All the application blanks used by them were numbered serially. They alone were authorized to sign receipts [1] for initiation fees received. Should other organizers wish to enroll members, as often happened at the monster mass meetings, they were given and charged with so many receipts duly signed by the secretaries. Later on they were required to return these receipts or three dollars apiece for them. The effect of all this was to make one man, and him bonded, responsible in each locality for all paper outstanding against the National Committee. This was abso-

[1] As a side light on organizing methods, it may be noted that the temporary receipts were red, white and blue cards. The patriotic foreigners were proud to carry these emblematic cards pending the time they got their regular cards. More than one man joined merely on that account.

[35]

lutely essential. No system was possible without this foundation.

The next step was definitely to fasten responsibility in the transfer of initiation fees from the local secretaries to the representatives of the various trade unions. To do so was most important. It was accomplished by requiring the local secretaries to exact from these men detailed receipts, specifying not only the amounts paid and the number of applications turned over, but also the serial number of each application. Bulk transfer of applications was prohibited, there being no way to identify the paper so handled.

The general effect of these regulations was to enable the National Committee almost instantly to trace any one of the thousands of applications continually passing through the hands of its agents. For instance, a steel worker who had joined at an office or a mass meeting, hearing later of the formation of his local union, would go to its meeting, present his receipt and ask for his union card. The secretary of the union would look up the applications which had been turned over to him. If he could not find one to correspond with the man's receipt he would take the matter up with the National Committee's local secretary. The latter could not deny his own signature on the receipt; he would have to tell what became of the application and the fee. On looking up the matter he would find that he had turned them over to a certain representative. Nor could the latter deny his signature on the detailed receipt. He would have to make good.

To facilitate the work, district offices were estab-

[36]

lished in Chicago and Youngstown. Organizers and secretaries held district meetings weekly. Local secretaries at points contiguous to these centers reported to their respective district secretaries. All others dealt directly with the general office of the National Committee.

It will be recalled that the co-operating unions, at the August 1–2 conference, agreed that the sum of one dollar should be deducted from each initiation fee for organization purposes. The collection of this money devolved upon the National Committee and presented considerable difficulty. It was solved by a system. The local secretaries, in turning over to the trades the applications signed up in their offices or at the mass meetings, held out one dollar apiece on them. For the applications secured at the meetings of the local unions they collected the dollars due with the assistance of blank forms sent to the unions. Each week the local secretaries sent reports to the general office of the National Committee, specifying in detail the number of members enrolled and turned over to the various trades, and enclosing checks to cover the amounts on hand after local expenses were met. These reports were duly certified by the representatives of the organizations involved, who signed their names on them at the points where the reports referred to the number of members turned over to their respective bodies. The whole system worked well.

Practical labor officials who have handled mass movements understand the great difficulties attendant upon the organization of large bodies of workingmen. In the steel campaign these were more serious than ever before. The tremendous number of men involved; their unfamiliarity with the English language and total lack of union experience; the wide scope of the operations; the complications created by a score of international unions, each with its own corps of organizers, directly mainly from far-distant headquarters; the chronic lack of resources; and the need for quick action in the face of incessant attacks from the Steel Trust — all together produced technical difficulties without precedent. But the foregoing systems went far to solve them. And into these systems the organizers and secretaries entered whole-heartedly. They realized that modern labor organizations cannot depend wholly upon idealism. They bore in mind that they were dealing with human beings and had to adopt sound principles of responsibility, standardization and general efficiency.

But another factor in the success of the campaign possibly even more important than the systems employed was the splendid morale of the organizers. A better, more loyal body of men was never gathered together upon this continent. They knew no such word as defeat. They pressed on with an irresistible assurance of victory born of their faith in the practicability of the theory upon which the campaign was worked out.

The organization of workingmen into trade unions is a comparatively simple matter when it is properly handled. It depends almost entirely upon the honesty, intelligence, power and persistence of the organizing forces. If these factors are strongly present, employers can do little to stop the move-

NATIONAL COMMITTEE DELEGATES

Youngstown, Ohio Meeting, Aug. 20, 1919.—Standing, left to right: F. P. Hanaway, *Miners*; D. Hickey, *Miners*; C. Claherty, *Blacksmiths*; R. J. Barr, *Machinists*; H. F. Liley, *Railway Carmen*; R. L. Hall, *Machinists*; R. T. McCoy, *Molders*; R. W. Beattie, *Firemen*; J. W. Morton, *Firemen*; P. A. Trant, *Amalgamated Association*. Seated, left to right: E. Crough, J. D. Cannon, *Mine, Mill and Smelter Workers*; F. J. Hardison, *Blacksmiths*; J. Manley, *Iron Workers*; Wm. Hannon, *Machinists*; John Fitzpatrick, *Chairman*; Wm. Z. Foster, *Sec.-Treasurer*; C. N. Glover, *Blacksmiths*; T. C. Cashen, *Switchmen*; D. J. Davis, *Amalgamated Association*.

ment of their employees. This is because the hard industrial conditions powerfully predispose the workers to take up any movement offering reasonable prospects of bettering their miserable lot. All that union organizers have to do is to place before these psychologically ripe workers, with sufficient clarity and persistence, the splendid achievements of the trade-union movement, and be prepared with a comprehensive organization plan to take care of the members when they come. If this presentation of trade unionism is made in even half-decent fashion the workers can hardly fail to respond. It is largely a mechanical proposition. In view of its great wealth and latent power, it may be truthfully said that there isn't an industry in the country which the trade-union movement cannot organize any time it sees fit. The problem in any case is merely to develop the proper organizing crews and systems, and the freedom-hungry workers, skilled or unskilled, men or women, black or white, will react almost as naturally and inevitably as water runs down hill.

This does not mean that there should be rosy-hued hopes held out to the workers and promises made to them of what the unions will get from the employers once they are established. On the contrary, one of the first principles of an efficient organizer is never, under any circumstances, to make promises to his men. From experience he has learned the extreme difficulty of making good such promises and also the destructive kick-back felt in case they are not fulfilled. The most he can do is to tell his men what has been done in other cases by organized workingmen and assure them that if they will stand to-

[39]

gether the union will do its utmost to help them. Beyond this he will not venture. And this position will enable him to develop the legitimate hope, idealism and enthusiasm which translates itself into substantial trade-union structure. The wild stories of extravagant promises made to the steel workers during their organization are pure tommyrot, as every experienced union man knows.

The practical effect of this theory is to throw on the union men the burden of responsibility for the unorganized condition of the industries. This is as it should be. In consequence, they tend to blame themselves rather than the unorganized men. Instead of indulging in the customary futile lamentations about the scab-like nature of the non-union man, "unorganizable industries," the irresistible power of the employers, and similar illusions to which unionists are too prone, they seek the solution of the problem in improvements of their own primitive organization methods.

This conception worked admirably in the steel campaign. It filled the organizers with unlimited confidence in their own power. They felt that they were the decisive factor in the situation. If they could but present their case strongly enough, and clearly enough to the steel workers, the latter would have to respond, and the steel barons would be unable to prevent it. A check or a failure was but the signal for an overhauling of the tactics used, and a resumption of the attack with renewed vigor. At times it was almost laughable. With hardly an exception, when the organizers went into a steel town to begin work, they would be met by the local union men and solemnly assured that it was utterly impossible to organize the steel mills in their town. " But," the organizers would say, " we succeeded in organizing Gary and South Chicago and many other tough places." " Yes, we know that," would be the reply, " but conditions are altogether different here. These mills are absolutely impossible. We have worked on them for years and cannot make the slightest impression. They are full of scabs from all over the country. You will only waste your time by monkeying with them." This happened not in one place alone, but practically everywhere — illustrating the villainous reputation the steel companies had built up as union smashers.

Side-stepping these pessimistic croakers, the organizers would go on to their task with undiminished self-confidence and energy. The result was success everywhere. The National Committee can boast the proud record of never having set up its organizing machinery in a steel town without ultimately putting substantial unions among the employees. It made little difference what the obstacles were; the chronic lack of funds; suppression of free speech and free assembly; raises in wages; multiplicity of races; mass picketing by bosses; wholesale discharge of union men; company unions; discouraging traditions of lost local strikes; or what not — in every case, whether the employers were indifferent or bitterly hostile, the result was the same, a healthy and rapid growth of the unions. The National Committee proved beyond peradventure of a doubt that the steel industry could be organized in spite of all the Steel Trust could do to prevent it.

Each town produced its own particular crop of problems. A chapter apiece would hardly suffice to describe the discouraging obstacles overcome in organizing the many districts. But that would far outrun the limits of this volume. A few details about the work in Johnstown will suffice to indicate the tactics of the employers and the nature of the campaign generally.

Johnstown is situated on the main line of the Pennsylvania railroad, seventy-five miles east of Pittsburgh. It is the home of the Cambria Steel Company, which employs normally from 15,000 to 17,000 men in its enormous mills and mines. It is one of the most important steel centers in America.

For sixty-six years the Cambria Company had reared its black stacks in the Conemaugh valley and ruled as autocratically as any mediæval baron. It practically owned the district and the dwellers therein. It paid its workers less than almost any other steel company in Pennsylvania and was noted as one of the country's worst union-hating concerns. According to old residents, the only record of unionism in its plants, prior to the National Committee campaign, was a strike in 1874 of the Sons of Vulcan, and a small movement a number of years later, in 1885, when a few men joined the Knights of Labor and were summarily discharged. The Amalgamated Association, even in its most militant days, was unable to get a grip in Johnstown. That town, for years, bore the evil reputation of being one where union organizers were met at the depot and given the alternative of leaving town or going to the lockup.

Into this industrial jail of a city the National Committee went in the early winter of 1918–19, at the invitation of local steel workers who had heard of the campaign. A. F. of L. organizer Thomas J. Conboy was placed in charge of the work. Immediately a strong organization spirit manifested itself — the wrongs of two-thirds of a century would out. It was interesting to watch the counter-moves of the company. They were typical. At first the officials contented themselves by stationing numbers of bosses and company detectives in front of the office and meeting halls to jot down the names of the men attending. But when this availed nothing, they took the next step by calling the live union spirits to the office and threatening them with dismissal. This likewise failed to stem the tide of unionism, and then the company officials applied their most dreaded weapon, the power of discharge. This was a dangerous course; the reason they did not adopt it before was for fear of its producing exactly the revolt they were aiming to prevent. But, all else unavailing, they went to this extreme.

Never was a policy of industrial frightfulness more diabolically conceived or more rigorously executed than that of the Cambria Steel Company. The men sacrificed were the Company's oldest and best employees. Men who had worked faithfully for ten, twenty or thirty years were discharged at a moment's notice. The plan was to pick out the men economically most helpless; men who were old and crippled, or who had large families dependent upon them, or homes half paid for, and make examples of them to frighten the rest. The case of

[43]

Wm. H. Seibert was typical; this man, a highly skilled mechanic, had worked for the Cambria Company thirty years. He was deaf and dumb, and could neither read nor write. He was practically cut off from all communication with his fellow workers. Yet the company, with fiendish humor, discharged him for being a union agitator. For every worker, discharge by the Cambria Company meant leaving Johnstown, if he would again work at his trade; for most of them it brought the severest hardships, but for such as Seibert it spelled ruin. With their handicaps of age and infirmities, they could never hope to work in steel mills again.

For months the Company continued these tactics.[1] Hundreds of union men were thus victimized. The object was to strike terror to the hearts of all and make them bow again to the mastery of the Cambria Steel Company. But the terrorists overshot the mark. Human nature could not endure it. They goaded their workers to desperation and forced them to fight back, however unfavorable the circumstances. The National Committee met in Johnstown and ordered a ballot among the men. They voted overwhelmingly to strike. A committee went to see Mr. Slick, the head of the Company, who refused to meet it, stating that if the men had any grievances they could take them up through the company union.

[1] In its war against unionism the Cambria Steel Company held nothing sacred, not even the church. During the campaign the Reverend George Dono Brooks, pastor of the First Baptist Church of Johnstown, took an active part, speaking at many meetings and generally lending encouragement to the workers. For this crime the company punished him by disrupting his congregation and eventually driving him from the city, penniless.

This company union played a large part in the drama of Johnstown. It was organized late in 1918 to forestall the trade unions. Such company unions are invariably mere auxiliaries to the companies' labor-crushing systems. They serve to delude the workers into believing they have some semblance of industrial democracy, and thus deter them from seeking the real thing. They consist merely of committees, made up for the most part of hand-picked bosses and "company suckers." There is no real organization of the workers. The men have no meetings off the property of the companies; they lack the advice of skilled trade unionists; they have no funds or means to strike effectively; they are out of touch with the workers in other sections of the industry. Consequently they have neither opportunity to formulate their grievances, nor power to enforce their adjustment. And little good would it do them if they had, for the lickspittle committees are always careful to see that they handle no business unless it relates to "welfare" work or other comparatively insignificant matters.

Company unions are invariably contemptible. All of them are cursed with company dictation, and all of them lack the vivifying principles of democratic control; but it is doubtful if a more degraded specimen can be found anywhere than that of the Cambria Steel Company. Without a murmur of protest it watched the company abolish the basic eight hour day late in 1918. Nor did it raise a finger to help the multitude of unfairly discharged union men. It habitually pigeonholed all real grievances submitted to it. But what else could be expected of a committee from which the company boldly discharged every man who dared say a word for the workers?

By referring the men's grievances to the despised company union, Mr. Slick only added fuel to the fire. A strike loomed threateningly, but just as it was about to break, Mr. Slick lost his job, presumably because of his unsuccessful labor policy. He was supplanted by A. A. Corey, Jr., formerly general superintendent of the Homestead Steel Works. Thinking perhaps the change in personnel might involve a change in policy, the committee approached Mr. Corey. He, too, refused to meet with it, stating publicly that the management would not deal with the representatives of outside organizations, but would take up the men's grievances, either through the company union, or " through any other accredited committee selected by the men in any way that is agreeable to them from among their own number." The last proposition was acceptable, and with joy the men held big open mass meetings of union and non-union men, and elected their committee. But their joy was short-lived. Mr. Corey, unashamed, wrote the committee that he had acted hastily before, and said, " I have had no previous experience with arrangements in the nature of collective bargaining, but a careful survey of this plan (company union), which I have since had time to make, convinces me that it makes full and complete provision for every contingency which can arise between the company and its employees." And then to make the men like this bitter medicine, the Company discharged an active member of the committee. All these events consumed many weeks and wore away the late winter and early spring months.

Mr. Corey's double-dealing provoked a fresh strike crisis; but by heroic measures the organizers repressed it. At all times a strike in Johnstown alone against the united steel companies was considered a move of desperation, a last resort to be undertaken only because nothing else could be done. But now relief was in sight. Spring was at hand and the national movement fast coming to a head. Its committees were knocking at the doors of the steel companies. The exposed and invaluable Johnstown position had to be held until this main army could come up and relieve it. So the Johnstown workers were told that they must refrain from counter-attacking, that they had to take all the blows heaped upon them and hold their ground at all costs.

And right nobly they did it. In spite of the bitterest hardships they built up and developed their organizations. In this they were unwittingly but powerfully aided by the company union. Several weeks before the big strike the officials took the hated general committee to Atlantic City, wined them and dined them and flattered them, as usual, and then had them adopt a set of resolutions condemning the national movement of the steel workers and endorsing long hours, low wages and heavier production as the remedy for prevailing bad conditions. This betrayal was the last straw. It provoked intense resentment among the men. Whole battalions of them, the most skilled and difficult in the plant to organize, walked down and joined the

[47]

unions in protest. Almost 3000 enrolled the week after the resolutions were adopted. But it was always thus. Every move that the Cambria made the unions turned to their advantage. They outgeneraled the Company at every turn.

It was almost pitiful to watch the later antics of the haughty and hitherto unchallenged Cambria Company, humbled in its own town by its own workers. A few weeks before Labor day .the unions, innocently presuming the mills would be closed as usual on that day, decided to have a parade. Then the strategical experts of the Company became active. A warning was issued that every man marching in the parade would be summarily discharged. The unions would not brook this unwarranted and cold-blooded attack. They promptly sent word to the Company that if a single man was discharged the whole plant would be stopped the next day. It was a clear-cut issue, and Johnstown held its breath. When Labor day came the city saw the biggest demonstration in its history. Fifteen thousand organized workers defied their would-be masters and marched. The Company swiftly backed water. And the next day not a man was discharged. It was a victory well worth the heroic efforts and suffering of the previous eight months.

When the great strike broke on September 22 the Johnstown workers went into the fight almost one hundred per cent. organized, and with about the same percentage of grievances. So few men were left in the plant that the Company had to ask the unions to give them help to shut down their furnaces, and to keep the fire protection in operation.

All the power of the great corporation, which had made $30,000,000 the year before, could not forestall the unions. It had no arrow in its quiver that could strike fear to the hearts of its workers; no trick in its brain pan that could be substituted for industrial democracy.

And Johnstown was only one point in the long battle line. Its experiences were but typical. Each steel town had its own bitter story of obstacles encountered and overcome. Youngstown, Chicago, Bethlehem, Cleveland, Wheeling, Pueblo, Buffalo and many other districts, each put up a hard fight. But one by one, despite all barriers, steel towns all over the country were captured for unionism.

V

BREAKING INTO PITTSBURGH

THE FLYING SQUADRON — MONESSEN — DONORA — McKEESPORT — RANKIN — BRADDOCK — CLAIR- TON — HOMESTEAD — DUQUESNE — THE RE- SULTS

THE time was now ripe for a great drive on Pitts- burgh, a district which had been the despair of unionism for a generation. The new strategy of the National Committee for Organizing Iron and Steel Workers was succeeding. Pittsburgh had been sur- rounded by organized posts, established during the winter. The Chicago district had also been held. The committee's finances were improving. The crew of organizers was larger and more enthusiastic than ever. The mills were operating stronger and stronger. And spring was here. The movement was now ready for a tremendous effort to capture Pittsburgh, and thus overcome, as far as might be, the original mistake of not starting the campaign soon enough and everywhere at the same time. This done, it would put the work squarely upon the essential national basis. So the assault was ordered on the stronghold of the Steel Trust.

First free speech and free assembly had to be established; for the towns about Pittsburgh were

[50]

still closed tight against the unions. During the winter incessant attempts had been made to break the embargo by political methods, but without avail. In vain a special convention of all the unions in Western Pennsylvania had appealed to the Governor for assistance. For a moment the federal Department of Labor displayed a languid interest and sent a dozen men to investigate conditions. But until this day their report has never appeared. In answer to inquiries, the Secretary of Labor is reported to have said that " its publication at this time would be inadvisable." That may be one reason, and another may be that the Department, in its eager co-operation with Attorney General Palmer, in deporting hundreds of workingmen without trials, is so busy that it hasn't time to attend to such trifles as the wholesale suppression of constitutional rights in Pennsylvania.

But in seeking relief no appeal was made to the courts to set up the rights of the unions. This was for two reasons. First, it would involve such a loss of time that the chance to organize the steel workers would have passed long before any decision could be secured. Then, again, there was no faith that the courts of Pennsylvania would be just, and the National Committee had no money to carry the fight higher. The unions conceived their rights to speak and assemble freely too well established to necessitate court sanction at this late date. Hence, they determined to exercise them, peacefully and lawfully, and to take the consequences. At Atlantic City, where the A. F. of L. was in convention, a dozen presidents of international unions in

[51]

the steel campaign expressed their willingness to enter the steel districts, to speak on the streets, and to go to jail if necessary.

To carry on the difficult and dangerous free speech fight, and to oversee generally the organization of the immediate Pittsburgh district, a special crew of organizers was formed. This was known as " The Flying Squadron," and was headed by J. L. Beaghen, A. F. of L. organizer and President of the Pittsburgh Bricklayers' Union. The following brief references to the fights in the various towns will illustrate the forces at play and the methods employed.

Monessen, forty miles from Pittsburgh on the Monongahela river, the home of the Pittsburgh Steel Company and several other large concerns, and notorious as the place where organizer Jeff. Pierce got his death blow in a previous campaign, was the first point of attack. Wm. Feeney, United Mine Workers' organizer and local secretary in charge of the district for the National Committee, superintended operations. Several months previously the Burgess of Monessen had flatly refused to allow him to hold any meetings in that town. So he was compelled to operate from Charleroi, several miles away. But as soon as spring peeped the question was opened again. He called a meeting to take place square in the streets of Monessen on April 1st. The Burgess forbade it with flaming pronunciamentos and threatened dire consequences if it were held. But Feeney went ahead, and on the date set marched 10,000 union miners from the surrounding country into Monessen to protest the suppression of free speech and free assembly. Mother Jones,[1] James Maurer, President of the Pennsylvania Federation of Labor, Philip Murray, President of District No. 5, U. M. W. A., Mr. Feeney, the writer and others spoke. The demonstration was a huge success. Public opinion was clearly on the side of the steel workers, and the Burgess had to recede from his dictatorial attitude and allow them to exercise their constitutional rights. This they hastened to do with gusto. The affair established the unions in the big mills of Monessen.

In Donora, an important steel town a few miles down the river from Monessen, and part of organizer Feeney's district, the fight was not so easily won. The United States Constitution provides that not even Congress may pass laws abridging the rights of free speech and free assembly; but in Pennsylvania the Constitution is considered a sort of humorous essay; hence the lickspittle Donora council, right in the face of the steel campaign, passed an ordinance forbidding public meetings without the sanction of the Burgess, which sanction, of course, the unions could not get. But nothing deterred, the indomitable Feeney hired a couple of lots on the edge of the town and held meetings there. The company officials left nothing undone to break up these gatherings. They held band concerts and ball games at

[1] Throughout the latter part of the organizing campaign and the first two months of the strike, Mother Jones lent great assistance to the steel workers. This veteran organizer (she testified in court to being 89 years old) of the United Mine Workers labored dauntlessly, going to jail and meeting the hardships and dangers of the work in a manner that would do credit to one half her age.

[53]

the same hour, and set dozens of their bosses and police to picket the meetings. But it was no use; the workers attended and joined the unions in droves.

This lasted a couple of months. And all the while a local paper was villainously assailing Feeney. Finally, the steel company agents got the business men to sign an ultimatum to Feeney, demanding that he leave the district at once. Feeney took this matter up with his miners, and they decided that not he, but they, would quit Donora. Organized solidly, they easily put a strict boycott on the town, and it was not long before the same business men, with their trade almost ruined, made a public apology to Feeney, and ousted their own officials who had been responsible for the attack.

Naturally these events heartened the steel workers. They organized very rapidly, and soon had a majority of the men in the mills — a large plant of the American Steel and Wire Company. They also became a big factor in the local fraternal associations, which controlled all the halls; and suddenly the Lithuanian Society deposed its President, who was friendly to the steel company, and voted to give its hall to the unions, permits or no permits. In the face of this situation the Burgess reluctantly granted sanction for union meetings. And thus free speech and free assembly were established in the benighted town of Donora, and with them, almost complete organization of the steel workers.

But the heart of the conspiracy against free speech and free assembly was in McKeesport, twenty miles from Pittsburgh. When the organizers tried to hold meetings in that city they could hire no halls without the Mayor's permission, and this the latter, George H. Lysle, stubbornly refused to give. He feared a revolution if the staid A. F. of L. unions were permitted to meet; but the Socialist party and other radical organizations went ahead with their gatherings without opposition. The truth was that he knew the unions would organize the workers if they could but get their ear, and this he determined to prevent. Nor would he shift from his autocratic position. Appeals by the organizers to the Federal government, the Governor and the local city council were alike fruitless. No meetings could be held in McKeesport. And the officials of all the steel towns along the Monogahela river, drawing inspiration from the little despot, Lysle, took the same stand. Free speech and free assembly were stifled in the whole district.

The Federal authorities being so active setting the outside world aright that they could find no time or occasion to correct the most glaring abuses at home, the unions resolved to attend to the free speech and free assembly matter themselves. Knowing that Lysle could knife the workers' rights only so long as he was allowed to work in the dark, they determined to drag him into the daylight and let the public judge of his deeds. They would hold meetings on the streets of McKeesport in spite of him; give him a few hundred test court cases to handle, and finally find out whether the A. F. of L. is entitled to the same rights as other organizations.

The fight opened as soon as the weather permitted. May 18 was the date set for the first meet-

[55]

ing. The Mayor stormed and threatened all concerned with instant arrest; but the preparations went on just the same. When the fated day arrived thousands turned out to hear the speakers. But the Mayor, failing to defend his course, dared not molest the meeting. After this, meetings were held on the streets each Sunday afternoon, always in the face of the Mayor's threats, until eventually the latter, seeing that he was the laughing stock of the city and that the street meetings were organizing hundreds of the workers, shamefacedly granted the following niggardly permit for meetings:

CITY OF McKEESPORT.

Department of Police.
McKeesport, Pa., July 7, 1919.

Mr. Reddington,
Chief of Police,
McKeesport, Pa.,
Dear Sir:

This is to certify that the McKeesport Council of Labor has permission to hold a mass meeting in Slavish Hall on White Street on July 8, 1919.

Permission is granted subject to the following conditions, and also subject to police regulation.

(1st) That no speaker shall talk in any other languages, except the English language.

(2nd) That a list of the speakers be submitted to the Mayor before the meeting is held.

Very truly yours,
(Signed)   Geo. H. Lysle
Mayor

Disregarding the three provisions of this contemptible document, the unions held their meetings under the auspices of the A. F. of L. (not of the McKeesport Council of Labor), had their speakers talk in whatever languages their hearers best understood, and submitted no list to Lysle. Then the big steel companies rushed to the aid of the hard-pressed Mayor. All the while they had discharged every man they could locate who had either joined the unions or expressed sympathy with them, but now they became more active. As each meeting was held they stationed about the hall doors (under the captaincy of Mr. William A. Cornelius, Manager of the National Tube Company's works) at least five hundred of their bosses, detectives, office help, and "loyal" workers to intimidate the men who were entering. About three hundred more would be sent into the hall to disrupt the meetings. And woe to the man they recognized, for he was discharged the next morning. The organizers, running the gauntlet of these Steel Trust gunmen, carried their very lives in their hands.

Under these hard circumstances few steel workers dared to go to the meetings or to the union headquarters. But the organizations grew rapidly nevertheless. Every discharged man became a volunteer organizer and busied himself getting his friends to enroll. A favorite trick to escape the espionage was to get a group of men, from a dozen to fifty, to meet quietly in one of the homes, fill out their applications, and send them by a sister or wife to the union headquarters — the detectives stationed outside naturally not knowing the women. Condi-

[57]

tions in the local mills were so bad that not even the most desperate employers' tactics could stop the progress of the unions. McKeesport quickly became one of the strong organization points on the river.

Sweeping onward through the Pittsburgh district, the unions gained great headway by the collapse of the petty Czar of McKeesport, for all the little nabobs in the adjoining steel towns felt the effects of his defeat. Rankin fell without a blow. A few months before the hall had been closed there by the local board of health, when the Burgess refused to act against the unions. But now no objections were made to the meetings. Braddock also capitulated easily. At a street meeting held in the middle of town against the Burgess' orders, organizers J. L. Beaghen, R. L. Hall, J. C. Boyle, J. B. Gent and the writer were arrested. The Burgess, however, not wishing to meet the issue, found it convenient to leave town, and the Acting Burgess, declaring in open court that he would not " do the dirty work of the Burgess," postponed the hearings indefinitely. That settled Braddock.

Burgess Williams of North Clairton, chief of the Carnegie mill police at that point, swore dire vengeance against the free speech fighters should they come to his town. But the National Committee, choosing a lot owned by its local secretary on the main street of North Clairton, called a meeting there one bright Sunday afternoon. But hardly had it started when, with a great flourish of clubs, the police broke up the gathering and arrested organizers J. G. Brown, J. Manley, A. A. Lassich, P. H.

Brogan, J. L. Beaghen, R. L. Hall, and the writer. Later all were fined for holding a meeting on their own property. But the Burgess, learning that the speaker for the following Sunday was Mother Jones of the Miners' Union, and that public sentiment was overwhelmingly against him, decided not to fight. Instead he provided a place on the public commons for open air meetings. The contest resulted in almost all of the local steel workers joining the unions immediately.

In Homestead, however, that sacred shrine of Labor, the unions had to put up a harder fight. The Burgess there, one P. H. McGuire, is a veteran of the great Homestead strike, and for many years afterwards led the local fight against the Carnegie Steel Company. But he has now fully recovered from his unionism. He has made peace with the enemy. It was in the early winter of 1918 that the unions first tried to hold meetings in his town. But they were careful to make tentative arrangements for a hall before asking a permit from McGuire. The latter stated flatly that there would be no union meetings in Homestead, saying no halls could be secured. " But," said the organizers, " we have already engaged a hall." The next day the rent money was returned with the explanation that a mistake had been made. Later the unions managed to sneak by the guard of the ex-union man Burgess and hold a meeting or two — said to be the first since the Homestead strike, twenty-six years before — but nothing substantial could be done, and the fight was called off for the winter.

During the big spring drive on Pittsburgh the

Flying Squadron turned its attention to Homestead as soon as the McKeesport and many other pressing situations permitted. Mass meetings were held on the main streets. At first the Burgess, with a weather eye on McKeesport, did not molest these; but when he saw the tremendous interest the steel workers showed and the rapidity with which they were joining the unions, he attempted to break up the meetings by arresting two of the organizers, J. L. Beaghen and myself. At the trial McGuire, as magistrate, was shown that his ordinance did not cover street meetings. "But," said he, "it's the best we've got, and it will have to do." He fined the defendants, and a day or two later had an ordinance adopted to his liking. Such trifles don't worry the executives in steel towns.

But such an enormous crowd assembled to witness the next street meeting that McGuire had to agree to permit hall meetings. No sooner were they attempted however, than he broke his agreement. He would allow no languages other than English to be spoken — the object being to prevent the foreign workers from understanding what was going on. Of course all other organizations in Homestead could use what tongues they pleased. The unions balked, with the result that more street meetings were held and Mother Jones, J. G. Brown, R. W. Reilly and J. L. Beaghen were arrested. Public indignation was intense; thousands marched the streets in protest; the unions grew like beanstalks. And so the affair went on till the great strike broke on September 22.

That curse of the campaign since its inception,

the lack of resources, bore down heavily on the work in the crucial summer months just before the strike. At least one hundred more men should have been put in the field to take advantage of the unparalleled opportunity. But the National Committee could not beg, borrow or steal them. The organizers in the various localities fairly shrieked for help, but in vain. Especially was the need keenly felt in the big drive on Pittsburgh. Instead of eight or ten men, which was all that the Flying Squadron could muster, there ought to have been at least fifty men delegated to the huge task of capturing the score of hard-baked steel towns on Pittsburgh's three rivers. The consequence was that the work everywhere had to be skimped, with disastrous effects later on in the strike. In those towns where the unions did get started lack of help prevented their taking full advantage of the situation. And then some towns had to be passed up altogether, although the men were infected with the general fever for organization and were calling for organizers. It was impossible to send any one to either Woodlawn or Midland, both very important steel towns. Even the strategic city of Duquesne, with its enormous mills and blast furnaces, could not be started until three weeks before the strike.

Duquesne is just across the river from McKeesport and only four miles from Homestead. It gave the organizers a hot reception. Its Mayor, James S. Crawford, is President of the First National Bank. His brother is President of the Port Vue Tinplate Company. Besides being Mayor, Mr. Crawford is city Commissioner, President of the city council, Director of Public Safety, and Magistrate. He makes the laws, executes them and punishes the violators. He is a true type of Pennsylvania steel town petty Kaiser and exercises his manifold powers accordingly.

So eager was the Mayor, popularly known as "Toad" Crawford, to give the world a demonstration of Steel Trust Americanism that he challenged the organizers to come to his town. He even offered to meet in personal combat one of the men in charge of the campaign. Of course he insultingly refused to grant permits for meetings. The organizers, who could not hire an office in the place, so completely were the property owners dominated by the steel companies, managed to lease a couple of lots in an obscure part of town. But when they attempted to hold a meeting there Mr. Crawford jailed three of them, J. L. Beaghen, J. McCaig, and J. G. Sause. The next day he fined them each $100 and costs.

Rabbi Wise of New York was the speaker billed for the following Sunday. But the Steel Trust Mayor forbade his meeting. And when it was proposed to have Frank Morrison, with whom Crawford boasted a slight acquaintance, confer with him about the situation, he declared, "It won't do you any good. Jesus Christ himself could not speak in Duquesne for the A. F. of L!" It so happened that Rabbi Wise was unable to come to Pennsylvania for his scheduled lectures on behalf of the steel workers, and the organizers held the Duquesne meeting themselves. Crawford had his whole police force on hand and immediately arrested the speakers, Mother Jones, J. L. Beaghen and the writer. Forty-four steel workers, all the jail would hold, were arrested also, foɩ no other reason than attending the meeting. Organizer J. M. Patterson, who had nothing to do with the gathering, was thrown into jail merely for trying to find out what bail we were held for. The next day the organizers were each fined $100 and costs, and the rest from $25 to $50 apiece.[1] In sentencing Mr. Beaghen, Mayor Crawford declared that nothing would be more pleasurable than to give him 99 years, and then be on hand when he got out to give him 99 more.

The Mayor was going it strong; but he was riding fast to a hard fall. The unions were planning to bring to Duquesne some of the most prominent men in the United States and to give Crawford the fight of his life, when the outbreak of the great strike swamped them with work and compelled them to turn their attention elsewhere.[2]

Whatever its general disadvantages, in some re-

[1] Relative to this meeting there occurs the following dialogue on page 508 of the report on the Senate Committee's Hearings on the Steel Strike:

Senator Sterling. "Was Mr. Foster here prior to the strike?"

Mr. Diehl (Gen. Manager Duquesne Works, Carnegie Steel Co.). "Yes; he was here trying to hold a meeting, but the meeting was not held."

The Chairman. "What happened to the meeting?"

Mr. Diehl. "Well, we simply prohibited it."

And naturally so. Mr. Diehl and other company officials shut off meetings in the halls and on the lots of their towns just as readily as they would have done had attempts been made to hold them in the mill yards.

[2] Now that the strike is over and spring is again at hand, the unions have resumed the battle for free speech and assembly in Duquesne and promise to fight it to a conclusion.

[63]

spects, at least, the free speech fight was very good for the unions. For one thing, it served wonderfully well to infuse the necessary hope and confidence into the steel workers. So tremendous had been the manifestations of the Steel Trust — its long record of victory over the trade unions, its vast wealth and undisputed political supremacy, its enormous mills and furnaces — so tremendous had been all these influences that they had overcome the individual workers with a profound sense of insignificance and helplessness, and practically destroyed all capacity for spontaneous action. What the steel men needed to rouse them from their lethargy was a demonstration of power from outside, a tangible sign that there was some institution through which they could help themselves. Throughout the campaign this consideration was borne in mind, and bands and other spectacular methods of advertising were used to develop among the steel workers a feeling of the greatness and power of the unions. Nor were these methods unsuccessful. Most effective of all, however, was the free speech fight in Pennsylvania. That gave the unions a golden opportunity to defeat the Steel Trust so easily and spectacularly that the steel workers couldn't help but be encouraged thereby. They simply had to cast in their lot with a movement able to defeat so handily their autocratic masters. And once they came in they felt the utmost confidence in their leaders, the men they had seen jailed time and again for fighting their battle.

In consequence of The Flying Squadron's heroic battles in the immediate Pittsburgh district the whole campaign was put practically upon a national basis,

[64]

where it should have been at the start. Almost every steel centre in America was being organized simultaneously. Members were streaming into the co-operating unions by thousands. The entire steel industry was on the move. Perhaps it may be fitting to introduce at this point an official digest of the general report of the number of men organized by the National Committee during the whole campaign. The report covers the period up to January 31, 1920, but almost all of the men were enrolled before the strike started on September 22.

GENERAL REPORT

on

250,000 members enrolled by the National Committee for Organizing Iron and Steel Workers during the American Federation of Labor Organizing Campaign in the Steel Industry, from August 1, 1918, until January 31, 1920.

By Localities		By Trades	
South Chicago	6,616	Blacksmiths	5,699
Chicago Heights	569	Boilermakers	2,097
Misc. Chicago Dist.	3,871	Brick & Clay Workers..	187
Pittsburgh	8,970	Bricklayers	581
Johnstown	11,846	Coopers	138
Butler	2,519	Electrical Workers	8,481
Monessen & Donora	8,665	Foundry Employees	2,406
New Castle	2,710	Hod Carriers	2,335
Homestead	3,571	Iron, Steel & Tin Wkrs..	70,026
Braddock & Rankin	4,044	Iron Workers	5,829
Clairton	2,970	Machinists	12,406
McKeesport	3,963	Metal Polishers	349
Gary	7,092	M. M. & Smelter Wkrs.	15,223
Indiana Harbor	4,654	Mine Workers	1,538
Joliet	3,497	Moulders	1,382
Milwaukee	681	Pattern Makers	....
Waukegan	1,212	Plumbers	1,369

By Localities		By Trades	
DeKalb	332	Quarry Workers	725
Aurora	242	Railway Carmen	5,045
Pullman	4,073	Seamen	....
Kenosha	585	Sheet Metal Workers	377
Hammond	1,102	Stationary Engineers	2,194
Wheeling Dist.	5,028	Stationary Firemen	5,321
Farrell & Sharon	3,794	Steam Shovelmen	2
Cleveland	17,305	Switchmen	440
Sparrows Point	93	Unclassified	12,552
Brackenridge & Natrona	2,110		
East Pittsburgh	146		
East Liverpool	50		
Warren & Niles	474		
Minnesota Dist.	185		
Pueblo	3,113		
Coatesville	828		
Steubenville Dist.	4,108		
Birmingham Dist.	1,470		
Canton & Massillon	5,705		
Vandergrift	1,986		
Buffalo & Lackawanna	6,179		
Youngstown	19,040		
Peoria	984		
Decatur	320		

Total by Localities...156,702   Total by Trades......156,702

This report includes only those members actually signed up by the National Committee for Organizing Iron and Steel Workers, and from whose initiation fees $1.00 apiece was deducted and forwarded to the general office of the National Committee. It represents approximately 50 to 60 per cent. of the total number of steel workers organized during the campaign, and is minimum in every respect.

The report does not include any of the many thousands of men signed up at Bethlehem, Steelton, Reading, Apollo, New Kensington, Leechburg and many minor points which felt the force of the drive but where the National Committee made no deductions upon initiation fees. In Gary, Joliet, Indiana Harbor, South Chicago and other Chicago District points the National Committee ceased collecting on initiation fees early in 1919, hence this report makes no showing of the thousands of men signed up in that territory during the last few months of the campaign. Likewise, at Coatesville and Sparrows' Point, during only a short space of the campaign were deductions made for the National Committee. Many thousands more men were signed up directly by the multitude of local unions in the steel industry, that were not reported to the National Committee. These do not show in this calculation. Nor do the great number of ex-soldiers who were taken into the unions free of initiation fees — in Johnstown alone 1300 ex-soldier steel workers joined the unions under this arrangement. Of course no accounting is here included for the army of workers in outside industries who became organized as a result of the tremendous impulse given by the steel campaign.

In view of these exceptions it may be conservatively estimated that well over 250,000 steel workers joined the unions notwithstanding the opposition of the Steel Trust, which discharged thousands of its workers, completely suppressed free speech and free assembly in Pennsylvania and used every known tactic to prevent the organization of its employees.

WM. Z. FOSTER,
Secretary-Treasurer
National Committee for Organizing
Iron & Steel Workers.

Certified by
    Enoch Martin
  Auditor, District No. 12
,United Mine Workers of America.

VI

STORM CLOUDS GATHER

RELIEF DEMANDED — THE AMALGAMATED ASSOCIA-
TION MOVES — A GENERAL MOVEMENT — THE
CONFERENCE COMMITTEE — GOMPERS' LETTER
UNANSWERED — THE STRIKE VOTE — GARY DE-
FENDS STEEL AUTOCRACY — PRESIDENT WILSON
ACTS IN VAIN — THE STRIKE CALL

SURGING forward to the accomplishment of the "impossible," the organization of the steel industry, the
twenty-four co-operating international unions found
themselves in grips with the employers long before
they were strong enough to sustain such a contest.
It is almost always so with new unions.   In their
infancy, when their members are weak, undisciplined
and inexperienced, and the employers are bitterly
hostile and aggressive, is exactly the time when they
must establish principles and adjust grievances that
would test the strength of the most powerful unions.
Inability to do so means dissolution, either through
a lost strike or by disintegration.   Following in the
wake of the newly formed steel workers' unions
came a mass of such difficulties requiring immediate
settlement.   The demand for relief from the evils

[68]

of long hours, low wages and miserable working conditions was bad enough; but infinitely more serious was the need to take care of the army of men discharged for union membership. Thousands of these walked the streets in the various steel towns clamoring for protection. And the men on the job demanded it for them. Nor could these appeals be ignored. Whether they deemed the occasion propitious or not, the steel workers' unions, on pain of extinction, had to act in defence of their harassed membership.

So bad was the situation by early spring that, lacking other means of relief, local strikes were threatening all over the country. To allow these forlorn-hope walkouts to occur would have meant disintegration and disaster to the whole campaign. They had to be checked at all costs and the movement kept upon a national basis. Therefore, the National Committee for Organizing Iron and Steel Workers called a general conference of delegates of steelworkers' unions of all trades through the entire industry, to take place in Pittsburgh, May 25, 1919. The object was to demonstrate to the rank and file how fast the national movement was developing, to turn their attention to it strongly, and thus hearten them to bear their hardships until it could come to their assistance.

Right in the face of this general movement of all the trades the Amalgamated Association made a bid for separate consideration by the steel companies. By instruction of its convention, President Tighe wrote the following letter to Mr. Gary:

[69]

Convention Hall, Louisville, Ky., May 15, 1919
Honorable Elbert H. Gary, Chairman,
Executive Officers, United States Steel Corporation,
Hoboken, N. J.
Dear Sir:

The Amalgamated Association of Iron, Steel and Tin Workers of North America, in National Convention assembled, have by resolution, instructed the undersigned to address you as Chairman of the Executive Officers of the United States Steel Corporation on a matter which in the opinion of the representatives of the Amalgamated Association of Iron, Steel and Tin Workers, is of vital importance to the Corporation you have the honor to represent and to the Amalgamated Association.

As you no doubt are aware, there is a serious disturbing element in the industrial world at the present time, a great spirit of unrest has spread over our common country. It is becoming more and more acute, and there is no telling when or where the storm clouds will break. It is the judgment of the representatives of the Amalgamated Association that it is the patriotic duty of all good citizens to use their every effort to stem the tide of unrest, if possible.

The Amalgamated Association of Iron, Steel and Tin Workers have admitted many thousands of the employees of the United States Steel Corporation into their organization; these members are asking that they be given consideration by the Corporation you are the Honorable Chairman of, in their respective crafts and callings, and also that as law-abiding citizens who desire the privilege of having their representatives meet with the chosen representatives of the Corporation you represent, to jointly confer on questions that mutually concern both.

Sincerely believing that the granting of their request

on your part will not only be the means of allaying that unrest, but will also promote and insure that harmony and co-operation that should at all times exist between employer and employee to the end that all will share in the glorious triumphs so lately achieved in the war and thereby add still more to the lustre and glory of our common country.

Trusting that you will give this request on the part of the aforesaid employees of your Corporation your most earnest consideration, I await your pleasure.

M. F. TIGHE, International President
Hotel Tyler, Louisville, Ky.

To this letter Mr. Gary replied as follows:

UNITED STATES STEEL CORPORATION

Chairman's Office,
New York, May 20th, 1919

Mr. M. F. Tighe,
International President,
Amalgamated Association of
Iron, Steel and Tin Workers,
Pittsburgh, Pa.
Dear Sir:

I have read with interest your letter of May 15th inst. I agree that it is the patriotic duty of all good citizens to use their efforts in stemming the tide of unrest in the industrial world whenever and wherever it exists.

As you know, we do not confer, negotiate with, or combat labor unions as such. We stand for the open shop, which permits a man to engage in the different lines of employment, whether he belongs to a labor union or not. We think this attitude secures the best results to the employees generally and to the employers.

In our own way, and in accordance with our best

[71]

judgment, we are rendering efficient patriotic service in the direction indicated by you.

With kind regards, I am,

Yours respectfully,

E. H. Gary, Chairman

The Amalgamated Association's action threatened the existence of the general movement, but Mr. Gary's refusal to deal with its officials kept them in the fold. Where the principle of solidarity was lacking outside pressure served the same end. It would be interesting to hear the Amalgamated Association officials explain this attempt at desertion.

At the conference of May 25 there assembled 583 delegates, representing twenty-eight international unions in eighty steel centers, the largest gathering of steel worker delegates in the history of the industry. The reports of the men present made it clearly evident that action had to be taken to defend the interests of their constituents. Consequently, disregarding the rebuff given the Amalgamated Association by Mr. Gary, the conference, which was only advisory in character, adopted the following resolution:

RESOLUTION

Whereas, We have now arrived at a point in our nation-wide campaign where our organizations control great numbers of the workers in many of the most important steel plants in America, and

Whereas, Various officials of the iron and steel industry, including Judge Gary, Charles Schwab, and other heads of these gigantic corporations have expressed their solicitude for the welfare of the workers in this industry, and

WHEREAS, They have been continuously quoted as defenders of the rights of the workers in industry, and

WHEREAS, The corporations, to block our progress, are organizing company unions, discharging union men wholesale and otherwise trying to break up our organization, thus compelling us to take action to escape destruction, therefore be it

RESOLVED, That it be the will of this conference that a joint effort be made by all unions affiliated with the National Committee for Organizing Iron and Steel Workers to enter into negotiations with the various steel companies to the end that better wages, shorter hours, improved working conditions and the trade-union system of collective bargaining be established in the steel industry; and be it further

RESOLVED, That this resolution be submitted for action to the National Committee for Organizing Iron and Steel Workers at its next meeting in Washington, D. C., May 27.

Two days later the National Committee met in Washington and adopted this resolution. The following were appointed as a conference committee to have charge of the preliminary negotiations with the steel companies: Samuel Gompers, Chairman of the National Committee; John Fitzpatrick, Acting Chairman; D. J. Davis, Amalgamated Association; Edw. J. Evans, Electrical Workers, Wm. Hannon, Machinists; Wm. Z. Foster, Railway Carmen. As the first approach, Mr. Gompers addressed the following letter to Mr. Gary, requesting a conference:

[73]

AMERICAN FEDERATION OF LABOR

The Alamac Hotel,
Atlantic City, N. J., June 20, 1919

Mr. Elbert H. Gary, Chairman,
Board of Directors, U. S. Steel Corporation,
New York, N. Y.

Dear Sir:

Of course you are aware that upon the request of a number of men in the employ of the United States Steel Corporation, and realizing the need of it, the convention of the American Federation of Labor decided to respond and give such assistance as is possible in order to bring about more thorough organization of the workers in the iron and steel industry, particularly those employed by your Corporation.

A campaign of organization was begun in June, 1918, and within that period we have secured the organization of more than 100,000 of the employees in the iron and steel industry. The prospects for the complete organization are, I am informed, exceedingly bright.

Of course, knowing the policy of the Organized Labor movement I have the honor in part to represent, we aim to accomplish the purposes of our labor movement; that is, better conditions for the toilers, by American methods, and American understandings, not by revolutionary methods or the inauguration of a cataclysm.

We believe in the effort of employer and employees to sit down around a table and, meeting thus, face to face, and having a better understanding of each other's position in regard to conditions of labor, to hours, standards, etc., and after reaching an amicable understanding to enter into an agreement for collective bargaining that is to cover wages, hours of labor, conditions of employment, etc.

At the Atlantic City convention of the American Federation of Labor just closed, the committee re-

[74]

ported upon the progress made, and I am instructed and authorized to suggest to you whether you will consent to hold a conference with a committee representing not only the iron and steel workers who are organized, but representing the best interests of the unorganized men in the employ of your Corporation. The names of the committee I am asking you to meet are:

Assistant President Davis, Amalgamated Iron and Steel and Tin Workers.

William Hannon, member executive board, International Association of Machinists.

Edward Evans, representing International Brotherhood of Electrical Workers.

Wm. Z. Foster, secretary of the National Committee for Organizing Iron and Steel Workers and representing the Brotherhood of Carmen of America.

John Fitzpatrick, president Chicago Federation of Labor.

If you can advise me at your early convenience that the request contained in this letter meets with your approval and that a conference can be held, I am sure I shall be additionally appreciative.

Kindly address your reply, which I trust may be favorable, to the American Federation of Labor Building, Washington, D. C.

Respectfully yours,
SAMUEL GOMPERS,
President American Federation of Labor

This letter was sent during the A. F. of L. convention at Atlantic City. About the same time Mr. Gompers resigned the chairmanship of the National Committee and appointed in his stead John Fitzpatrick, hitherto Acting Chairman. Mr. Fitzpatrick has been President of the Chicago Federation of Labor for many years. He is a horseshoer by trade and one of America's sterling union men. Possessed of a broad idealism, unquestioned integrity, a magnetic personality and a wide knowledge of trade-union practice, his services were beyond value as Chairman of the committees that carried on the organization work in the steel and packing industries. He is now taking an active part in the launching of the new Labor party.

To Mr. Gompers' courteous letter Czar Gary did not deign to reply. This was bad. It looked like war. But the unions had no alternative; they had to go ahead. Conditions in the steel industry were so unbearable that they had to exert their utmost power to right them, come what might. Therefore, after waiting several weeks for word from Mr. Gary, the National Committee met, gave the situation profound consideration, and adopted the following resolution:

RESOLUTION

WHEREAS, Working conditions in the steel industry are so intolerable and the unrest arising therefrom so intense that they can only be remedied by the application of the principles of collective bargaining; and,

WHEREAS, All efforts have failed to bring about a conference between the heads of the great steel corporations and the trade unions, representing many thousands of organized steel workers, for the purpose of establishing trade union conditions in the steel industry; therefore, be it

RESOLVED, That the National Committee for Organizing Iron and Steel Workers recommends to its 24 affiliated unions that they take a strike vote of their local unions throughout the steel industry; and, be it further

RESOLVED, That a special meeting be held in the

[76]

Pittsburgh Labor Temple, July 20th, at 10 A. M., of representatives of all the co-operating international unions for the purpose of taking action on this matter.

The National Committee meeting of July 20th, called in accordance with the above resolution, approached the situation from every possible angle and with the keenest sense of responsibility. But it had to recognize that the matter was wholly in the hands of Mr. Gary and his associates. The resolution to take a strike vote of the men was re-adopted. Also the following general demands, based on accurate surveys of the situation, and subject to revision over the conference table, were formulated:

1. Right of collective bargaining
2. Reinstatement of all men discharged for union activities with pay for time lost
3. Eight hour day
4. One day's rest in seven
5. Abolition of 24-hour shift
6. Increases in wages sufficient to guarantee American standard of living
7. Standard scales of wages in all trades and classifications of workers
8. Double rates of pay for all overtime after 8 hours, holiday and Sunday work
9. Check-off system of collecting union dues and assessments
10. Principles of seniority to apply in the maintenance, reduction and increase of working forces
11. Abolition of company unions
12. Abolition of physical examination of applicants for employment

So plain, fair and equitable are these demands that

to reasonable people they require no defence. The only explanation they might need relates to #9 and #12. The check-off was to apply only to the mining end of the steel industry, and the abolition of the physical examination was to put a stop to the rank discrimination practiced by the companies through their medical departments.

A month was allowed in which to take the vote. Each trade looked after its own members, with the National Committee voting those men who were enrolled but not yet turned over to their respective unions, and in some cases the unorganized also. Enthusiasm was intense. The steel workers saw a glimmer of hope and welcomed with open arms the opportunity to right their crying wrongs. When the vote was tabulated in Youngstown, Ohio, on August 20, it was found that every trade had voted overwhelmingly for a strike in case no settlement could be reached. Whole districts voted to a man in the affirmative. Of all the thousands of ballots cast in Homestead, Braddock, Rankin, McKeesport, Vandergrift, Pittsburgh and Monessen not one was in the negative. Donora produced one " no " vote, with the great Youngstown, Chicago and Cleveland districts about the same. Everywhere the sentiment was practically unanimous to make a stand. The vote was calculated conservatively at 98 per cent. for a strike. The Conference Committee was accordingly instructed to request a conference with the heads of the United States Steel Corporation and the big independent companies, and if at the end of ten days no such meeting had been arranged, to set the strike date.

BlackSmith

BALLOT

IRON & STEEL WORKERS

The Union Committees are now seeking to get higher wages, shorter hours and better working conditions from the steel companies. Are you willing to back them up to the extent of stopping work should the companies refuse to concede these demands?

TAJNO GLASANJE

Odbor junije sada traži da se dobije bolja plaća, kraći radni satovi i bolji uvjeti za rad od kompanija čelika. Dali ste voljni isti do skrajnosti podupreti da se prestane sa radom ako bi kompanija odbila da udovolji zahtevima?

SZAVAZZON!

Az Union Bizottsága, az Acél Társaságoktól való—magasabb fizetés, rövidebb munka idő és jobb munka feltételek—elnyerése után törekszik. Akar ezek után törekedni? s a végsökig kitarta—ni? és ha a társaságok ezen kivánalmaknak nem tesznek eleget a munkát beszüntetni?

VOTAZIONE.

I comitati dell'Unione stanno cercando di ottenere paghe piu' alte, ore di lavoro piu' brevi, e migliori condizioni di lavoro. Desiderate voi assecondarli, anche quando dovesse essere necessario di fermare il lavoro se le Compagnie rifiutassero di accettare le domande?

HLÁSOVACI LÍSTOK

Výbor uniový chce dosiahnuť podvýšenie mzdy, menej hodín robiť a lepšie robotnícke položenie od oceliarskych spoločností. Ste vy ochotní ich podporovať do krajnosti, až do zástavenia práce, v páde by spoločnosť odoprela žiadosťučiniť tým požiadavkám.

BALOT

Komitet Unii stara się obecnie o uzyskanie od Stalowych Kompanij większej płacy, krótszych godzin i lepszych warunków pracy. Czy jesteś gotów poprzeć nas aż do możliwości wstrzymania pracy na wypadek, gdyby Kompanie odmówiły naszym żądaniom?

VOTE YES OR NO.   Mark X in square indicating how you vote

IPEU   Yes [X]   No [ ]

National Committee for Organizing Iron and Steel Workers

WM. Z. FOSTER, Secy-Treas.   303 Magee Bldg., Pittsburgh, Pa.

9

STRIKE BALLOT

Taking no further chances on unanswered letters, the Committee bearded Mr. Gary in his lair at 71 Broadway. He was in but refused to meet the Committee, requesting that its proposition be submitted in writing. The Committee thereupon sent him the following request for a conference:

New York, August 26, 1919

Hon. Elbert H. Gary, Chairman Finance Committee,
United States Steel Corporation,
71 Broadway, New York City

Dear Sir:

During a general campaign of organization and education conducted under the auspices of the American Federation of Labor, many thousands of men employed in the iron and steel industry made application and were enrolled as members of the various organizations to which they were assigned.

This work has been carried on to a point where we feel justified in stating to you that we represent the sentiment of the vast majority of the employees in this industry, and, acting in behalf of them, we solicit of you that a hearing be given to the undersigned Committee, who have been selected by the duly accredited representatives of the employees, to place before you matters that are of vital concern to them, and concerning hours of labor, wages, working conditions and the right of collective bargaining.

The committee called at your office at 3 P. M., Tuesday, August 26, and requested a conference. We were advised by your messenger that you wished to be excused from a personal interview at this time and requested us to have our business in writing and whatever matters we wished to submit would be taken up by yourself and your colleagues and given consideration.

Therefore we are submitting in brief the principal

[79]

subjects that we desired to have a conference on. The committee has an important meeting in another city on Thursday next and will leave New York at 5 o'clock on August 27, 1919. May we respectfully request that your answer be sent before that time to Mr. John Fitzpatrick, Continental Hotel, Broadway and Forty-first Street, New York City.

Very truly yours,
John Fitzpatrick
D. J. Davis
Wm. Hannon
Edw. J. Evans
Wm. Z. Foster
Committee

To this letter Mr. Gary replied as follows:

UNITED STATES STEEL CORPORATION

Office of the Chairman,
New York, August 27, 1919

Messrs. John Fitzpatrick, David J. Davis, William Hannon, Wm. Z. Foster, Edw. J. Evans, Committee
Gentlemen:

Receipt of your communication of August 26 instant is acknowledged.

We do not think you are authorized to represent the sentiment of a majority of the employees of the United States Steel Corporation and its subsidiaries. We express no opinion concerning any other members of the iron and steel industry.

As heretofore publicly stated and repeated, our Corporation and subsidiaries, although they do not combat labor unions as such, decline to discuss business with them. The Corporation and subsidiaries are opposed to the " closed shop." They stand for the " open shop," which permits one to engage in any line of employment whether one does or does not belong to a labor union. This best promotes the welfare of both employees and employers. In view of the well-known attitude as above expressed, the officers of the Corporation respectfully decline to discuss with you, as representatives of a labor union, any matter relating to employees. In doing so no personal discourtesy is intended.

In all decisions and acts of the Corporation and subsidiaries pertaining to employees and employment their interests are of highest importance. In wage rates, living and working conditions, conservation of life and health, care and comfort in times of sickness or old age, and providing facilities for the general welfare and happiness of employees and their families, the Corporation and subsidiaries have endeavored to occupy a leading and advanced position among employers.

It will be the object of the Corporation and subsidiaries to give such consideration to employees as to show them their loyal and efficient service in the past is appreciated, and that they may expect in the future fair treatment.

Respectfully yours,
E. H. GARY, Chairman

In a last effort to prevail upon Mr. Gary to yield his tyrannical position, the committee addressed him this further communication:

New York City, Aug. 27, 1919.

Hon. Elbert H. Gary, Chairman
    Finance Committee, United States Steel Corporation,
        71 Broadway, New York, N. Y.
Dear Sir:
We have received your answer to our request for a conference on behalf of the employees of your Corporation, and we understand the first paragraph of your answer to be an absolute refusal on the part of your

corporation to concede to your employees the right of collective bargaining.

You question the authority of our committee to represent the majority of your employees. The only way by which we can prove our authority is to put the strike vote into effect and we sincerely hope that you will not force a strike to prove this point.

We asked for a conference for the purpose of arranging a meeting where the questions of wages, hours, conditions of employment, and collective bargaining might be discussed. Your answer is a flat refusal for such conference, which raises the question, if the accredited representatives of your employees and the international unions affiliated with the American Federation of Labor and the Federation itself are denied a conference, what chance have the employees as such to secure any consideration of the views they entertain or the complaints they are justified in making.

We noted particularly your definition of the attitude of your Corporation on the question of the open and closed shop, and the positive declaration in refusing to meet representatives of union labor. These subjects are matters that might well be discussed in conference. There has not anything arisen between your Corporation and the employees whom we represent in which the question of " the closed shop " has been even mooted.

We read with great care your statement as to the interest the Corporation takes in the lives and welfare of the employees and their families, and if that were true even in a minor degree, we would not be pressing consideration, through a conference, of the terrible conditions that exist. The conditions of employment, the home life, the misery in the hovels of the steel workers is beyond description. You may not be aware that the standard of life of the average steel worker is below the pauper line, which means that charitable institutions furnish to the pauper a better home, more food, clothing, light and heat than many steel workers can bring into their lives upon the compensation received for putting forth their very best efforts in the steel industry. Surely this is a matter which might well be discussed in conference.

You also made reference to the attitude of your Corporation in not opposing or preventing your employees from joining labor organizations. It is a matter of common knowledge that the tactics employed by your Corporation and subsidiaries have for years most effectively prevented any attempt at organization by your employees. We feel that a conference would be valuable to your Corporation for the purpose of getting facts of which, judging from your letter, you seem to be misinformed.

Some few days are still at the disposal of our committee before the time limit will have expired when there will be no discretion left to the committee but to enforce the decree of your employees whom we have the honor to represent.

We submit that reason and fairness should obtain rather than that the alternative shall be compulsory upon us.

Surely reasonable men can find a common ground upon which we can all stand and prosper.

If you will communicate with us further upon this entire matter, please address your communication to the National Hotel, Washington, D. C., where we will be Thursday and Friday, August 28 and 29.

Very truly yours,

JOHN FITZPATRICK
D. J. DAVIS
WM. HANNON
EDW. J. EVANS
WM. Z. FOSTER
Committee

No reply came to the last letter. Mr. Gary, behind the smoke screen of his hypocrisies about the " open shop," was determined to have the strike go on. But the committee, fully conscious of the tremendous responsibility resting upon it, was equally decided to exhaust every possible means of adjustment before things came to a rupture. The committeemen went to Washington, appeared before the Executive Council of the A. F. of L., and received its endorsement and praise for the manner in which the campaign had been conducted.

Mr. Gompers was delegated by the Council to go with the committee to present the matter to President Wilson, and to request him to arrange a conference with the steel people.

When President Wilson was informed of the true situation in the steel industry, that all the men were asking for was a conference at which to present their grievances — absolutely no other demand having been made upon Mr. Gary — he immediately admitted the justice of the committee's position. He stated frankly that he was entirely out of sympathy with employers who refused to meet with representatives of their workers for the purpose of bargaining collectively on labor conditions, and he definitely agreed to use all his influence privately to have Mr. Gary alter his decision and to arrange the conference. In order to give him a chance to work the unions withheld the setting of the strike date.

A week passed, with no word from the President. Conditions in the steel industry were frightful. The companies, realizing the importance of striking the first blow, were discharging men by the thousands.

The unions could wait no longer. They had to move or be annihilated. On September 4, the National Committee met and sent to President Wilson, who was on his ill-starred trip through the West advocating the League of Nations, the following telegram, in the meantime calling a meeting of the Presidents of all the international unions co-operating in the steel campaign to consider the critical situation:

Washington, September 4, 1919

Honorable Woodrow Wilson,
    President of the United States,
        Indianapolis, Ind., *en route*

The Executive Committee representing the various international unions in the iron and steel industry met today to consider the awful situation which exists in many of the iron and steel industry centres. The coercion, the brutality employed to prevent men and unions from meeting in halls engaged, upon private property, in the open air, the thuggery of the Corporations' emissaries, the wholesale discharge of numbers of men for no other reason than the one assigned, that they have become members of the unions, have brought about a situation such that it is exceedingly difficult to withhold or restrain the indignation of the men and the resistance they declare it is their purpose to present. The Executive Committee, relying upon the case as presented to you last week and your earnest declaration to endeavor to bring about a conference for the honorable and peaceful adjustment of the matters in controversy, have thus far been enabled to prevail upon the men not to engage in a general strike. We cannot now affirm how much longer we will be able to exert that influence; but we urge you, in the great work in which you are engaged, to give prompt attention to this most vital of

[85]

issues; for if the men can no longer be restrained it is impossible to foretell what the future may hold in store for an industrial crisis which may ensue and frustrate the project which you have worked at for a peaceful and honorable adjustment of industrial affairs in our country. A meeting of all the Presidents of the twenty-four international unions in the steel industry has been called to take place on Tuesday, September 9th in Washington, D. C. to take such action as they deem necessary. May we not have your reply on or before that time as to whether or not a conference with the Steel Corporation is possible.

SAMUEL GOMPERS
JOHN FITZPATRICK
D. J. DAVIS
WM. HANNON
EDW. J. EVANS
WM. Z. FOSTER

The international presidents met on September 9. A telegram from Secretary Tumulty was laid before them, to the effect that President Wilson had not yet been successful in arranging the requested conference; that he was somewhat discouraged, but was continuing his efforts. The general opinion took this to be final, that Mr. Gary had definitely refused the President's request. But in order to make assurance doubly sure and to convine all involved that everything possible had been done to avert a break, the following further telegram was sent to Mr. Wilson, over the objections of some who felt it was practically asking him to declare the strike:

Washington, September 9, 1919

Honorable Woodrow Wilson,
   President of the United States,
      St. Paul Hotel,
         St. Paul, Minnesota

Secretary Tumulty's telegram of September fifth to Samuel Gompers was read today at the meeting of the presidents of the twenty-four international unions in the steel industry, and given the most careful consideration. After a long and earnest discussion of it the undersigned were instructed to wire you requesting a more definite statement as to the possibility of an early conference being arranged by your efforts between the heads of the United States Steel Corporation and of the unions involved. Large numbers of men are being discharged and otherwise discriminated against and abused, and it will be impossible to hold our men much longer from defending themselves by striking unless some genuine relief is vouchsafed them. Our meeting will remain in session here for forty-eight hours awaiting your reply before taking final action. Please send answer to John Fitzpatrick, Chairman of National Committee, American Federation of Labor Building, Washington, D. C.

JOHN FITZPATRICK
M. F. TIGHE
WM. HANNON
WM. Z. FOSTER

On the day following Secretary Tumulty's answer was laid on the table before the meeting, practically repeating what his first telegram had said. It held out no definite hope for a conference, neither did it suggest any alternative.[1] Clearly the unions had to

[1] Out of courtesy to the President the National Committee has never made public these telegrams.

act. President Gompers and others had warned of the great power of the Steel Trust and the eagerness with which the employing class would unite to give Organized Labor a heavy blow in the steel industry. The union representatives keenly realized the gravity of the situation and their heavy responsibilities. It was in this frame of mind that they could see no honorable way out of the difficulty except to strike. Accordingly President Tighe of the Amalgamated Association moved that the strike be set for September 22. His motion was unanimously adopted. The die was cast. After telegraphing the strike order broadcast, the union men scattered to their respective posts to organize the walkout.

Then came a bolt from the blue. Next morning the newspapers carried a telegram from Secretary Tumulty to President Gompers requesting that the strike be held off until after the Industrial conference, beginning October 6. The committeemen could hardly believe their eyes, because the telegram they had received from Mr. Tumulty had said absolutely nothing about postponing the strike. Besides, since the President had asked Mr. Gary privately to grant his workers the conference they were seeking, and so gave him an opportunity to decline without publicity, it was incredible that he would publicly make a request upon the unions which involved their destruction, and which they would have openly to refuse, thus putting them in a bad light and giving their opponents a powerful weapon. But all doubts were set at rest by this communication from Mr. Gompers:

AMERICAN FEDERATION OF LABOR

Washington, D. C., Sept. 11, 1919

Mr. John Fitzpatrick, Chairman,
 National Committee For Organizing Iron
   and Steel Workers,
 Washington, D. C.,

Dear Mr. Fitzpatrick:

This morning I received a telegram as follows:

Dickinson, N. Dak., Sept. 10, 1919

Hon. Samuel Gompers,
 President American Federation of Labor,
   Washington, D. C.

In view of the difficulty of arranging any present satisfactory mediation with regard to the steel situation, the President desires to urge upon the steel men, through you, the wisdom and desirability of postponing action of any kind until after the forthcoming Industrial conference at Washington. J. P. TUMULTY.

You are aware of the reason which prevented my participating further, the past few days, in the conferences with the representatives of the various national and international unions involved in this question.

In transmitting the above to you (which I am doing by long distance telephone from New York) I want to express the hope that something can be done without injury to the workers and their cause to endeavor to conform to the wish expressed by the President; that even though the corporations may endeavor to provoke the men to action, that they may hold themselves in leash and under self-control, consciously demonstrating their stamina and willingness to abide by the justice of their cause and that their rights will be finally protected. Fraternally yours,

SAMUEL GOMPERS,
President
American Federation of Labor
[89]

Upon the receipt of this letter a meeting of the National Committee was at once called to consider the situation. And a serious one it was indeed. Before the Committee lay two requests to postpone the strike; one from President Wilson, clear and categoric; the other from Mr. Gompers, qualified by the hope that it could be done " without injury to the workers and their cause." To deny these powerful requests meant to be accused, in the first instance, of hasty and disloyal action, and in the second, of practical revolt against the officials of the A. F. of L. It would be to start the strike under the handicap of an unduly hostile public opinion. Yet to grant them meant ruin complete.

Conditions in the steel industry were desperate. Everywhere the employers were making vigorous attacks on the unions. From Chicago, Youngstown, Newcastle, Steubenville, Wheeling, Buffalo, Pittsburgh, and many other points large numbers of men were being thrown out of work because of their union membership. Johnstown was a bleeding wound. In the towns along the Monongahela river thousands of discharged men walked the streets, and their number was daily being heavily increased.

In the face of this situation it would have been folly to have the steel workers abandon their strike preparations, even if it could have been done. It was like asking one belligerent to ground arms in the face of its onrushing antagonist. The employers gave not the slightest sign of a truce. Long before anything could be hoped for from the Industrial conference, they would have cut the unions to pieces,

[90]

had the workers been foolish enough to give them the opportunity.

This the steel workers were determined not to do. Immediately after the story got abroad that the strike might be postponed, they met in their unions and notified the National Committee that they were going to strike on September 22, regardless of anything that body might do short of getting them definite concessions and protection. Many long weary months they had waited patiently, under the urgings of the organizers, for a chance to redress their grievances. And now when they had built their organizations; taken their strike vote; received their strike call and were ready to deliver a blow at their oppressors, the opportunity of a generation was at hand, and they were not going to see it lost. They would not postpone indefinitely, and in all likelihood break up altogether, the movement they had suffered so much to build, in the vague hope that the Industrial conference, which they had no guarantee would even consider their case, and which was dominated by their arch enemies, Gary and Rockefeller, would in some distant day do something for them. Their determination to have the strike go on was intensified by the constant ding-donging of the Steel Trust propaganda in the mills to the effect that the A. F. of L. unions were cowardly and corrupt; that they would make no fight for the steel workers, and that a postponement of the strike would be proof positive that they had sold out. Under such circumstances the workers could not consent to the withholding of the strike. Practically all the steel dis-

[91]

tricts in the country solemnly warned the National Committee that they would strike on September 22, in spite of any postponement that was not based on positive assurances that justice would be done. The control of the situation was in the hands of the rank and file.

The field secretaries and organizers present at the National Committee meeting, men intimately acquainted with actual conditions, emphasized the impossibility of postponement. Many of them, among whom were some of the best and most conservative men in the whole campaign, declared that an attempt to delay the strike, merely upon the strength of possible action by the Industrial conference, would result in the swift destruction of the movement under the worst of circumstances. The workers would be bound to consider it a gigantic sell-out and to act acordingly. As for themselves, they declared they would have nothing to do with it, and would be compelled to present their resignations the minute a motion to postpone prevailed. Dozens of them took this stand.

To the National Committee two courses were open: (1) It could postpone the strike with the absolute certainty that it would break the steel movement by so doing, because the strike would have gone ahead anyway in a series of wild, uncontrolled, leaderless revolts, waged in an atmosphere fatally charged with accusations of cowardice and graft. In all probability the A. F. of L. would suffer one of the worst defeats in its history, and gain such an evil reputation among the steel workers that it could not approach them for many years, if ever, with an organization project. Or (2) it could go ahead with the strike, with a fighting chance to win. In any event, even if the strike were lost, it would be through a clean fight and the honor of the movement would be preserved. The steel workers would be convinced that everything possible had been done for them. Thus the unions would retain their confidence and be enabled to re-organize them at an early date.

Between certain, ignominious defeat and possible victory, or at the worst honorable failure, the National Committee had only one choice. Practically all the delegates present were of the opinion that the strike had to go on. But some had to wire their international offices to cancel their instructions to vote for postponement. On September 18, D. J. Davis, Assistant President of the Amalgamated Association moved that September 22 be reaffirmed as the strike date. This was carried.[1] Then the Conference Committee addressed a long letter to President Wilson, explaining in detail the situation as the union men saw it and outlining the reasons for not

[1] After he had been made fully acquainted with the situation Mr. Gompers said before the Senate Committee on Education and Labor, investigating the steel strike: (Hearings, page 109) "Notwithstanding what any of the officials of the trade unions would have done, regardless of what the Committee would have done, the strike would have occurred anyway, a haphazard, loose, disjointed, unorganized strike, without leadership, without consultation, without advice. It was simply a choice whether the strike would take place under the guidance and leadership of men who have proven their worth, or under the leadership of some one who might spring up for the moment."

postponing the strike.   The letter closed as follows:

> Mr. President, delay is no longer possible.   We have tried to find a way but cannot.   We regret that for the first time your call upon Organized Labor cannot meet with favorable response.   Believe us the fault is not ours.   If delay were no more than delay, even at the cost of loss of membership in our organizations, we would urge the same to the fullest of our ability, notwithstanding the men are set for an immediate strike.   But delay here means the surrender of all hope.   This strike is not at the call of the leaders, but that of the men involved.   Win or lose, the strike is inevitable and will continue until industrial despotism will recede from the untenable position now occupied by Mr. Gary.   We have faith in your desire to bring about a conference and hope you will succeed therein.   We fully understand the hardships that meanwhile will follow and the reign of terror that unfair employers will institute.   The burden falls upon the men, but the great responsibility therefor rests upon the other side.

After agreeing that all settlements made with the employers should cover all trades, and sending a letter to the independent steel companies inviting conferences with them, the meeting adjourned and the organizers and delegates left to make good the following strike call, of which 200,000 copies, in seven languages, had been scattered broadcast throughout the entire steel industry:

STRIKE SEPTEMBER 22, 1919

The workers in the iron and steel mills and blast furnaces, not working under union agreements, are requested not to go to work on September 22, and to refuse to resume their employment until such time as the demands of the organizations have been conceded by the steel corporations.

The union committees have tried to arrange conferences with the heads of the steel companies in order that they might present our legitimate demands for the right of collective bargaining, higher wages, shorter hours and better working conditions. But the employers have steadfastly refused to meet them. It therefore becomes our duty to support the committees' claims, in accordance with the practically unanimous strike vote, by refusing to work in the mills on or after September 22, until such time as our just demands have been granted. And in our stoppage of work let there be no violence. The American Federation of Labor has won all its great progress by peaceful and legal methods.

IRON AND STEEL WORKERS! A historic decision confronts us. If we will but stand together now like men our demands will soon be granted and a golden era of prosperity will open for us in the steel industry. But if we falter and fail to act this great effort will be lost, and we will sink back into a miserable and hopeless serfdom. The welfare of our wives and children is at stake. Now is the time to insist upon our rights as human beings.

STOP WORK SEPTEMBER 22
NATIONAL COMMITTEE
FOR ORGANIZING IRON AND STEEL WORKERS.

VII

THE STORM BREAKS

THE STEEL TRUST ARMY — CORRUPT OFFICIALDOM — CLAIRTON — McKEESPORT — THE STRIKE — SHOWING BY DISTRICTS — A TREASONABLE ACT — GARY GETS HIS ANSWER

As the memorable twenty-second of September approached a lurid and dramatic setting developed for the beginning of the great steel strike. Everywhere the steel companies made gigantic preparations to crush their aspiring workers back to slavery. The newspapers shrieked revolution. The whole country was a-tremble with anxiety and apprehension.

Pittsburgh was the storm center. There, in its stronghold, the Steel Trust went ahead with strike-breaking measures unprecedented in industrial history. It provisioned and fortified its great mills and furnaces, surrounding them with stockades topped off with heavily charged electric wires, and bristling with machine guns. It assembled whole armies of gunmen. Brute force was to be used in breaking the solidarity of the workers. Said the New York *World* editorially September 22: "In anticipation of the steel strike, what do we see? In the Pittsburgh district thousands of deputy sheriffs have been recruited at several of the

[96]

larger plants. The Pennsylvania State Constabulary has been concentrated at commanding points. At other places the authorities have organized bodies of war veterans as special officers. At McKeesport alone 3,000 citizens have been sworn in as special police deputies subject to instant call. It is as though preparations were made for actual war."

Along the Monongahela river from Pittsburgh to Clairton, a distance of twenty miles, there were not less than 25,000 armed men in the service of the Steel Trust. In the entire Pittsburgh district, practically all the petty parasites who prey upon the steel workers — the professional and small business men — had been sworn in as deputies and furnished firearms to defend their great overlord, to whom they all do unquestioning service no matter how dirty the job. During the strike Sheriff Haddock of Allegheny county stated to the Senate Committee investigating the strike that there were 5,000 deputy sheriffs and 5,000 strikers in his jurisdiction, or one deputy for each striker. His totals should have been multiplied by at least ten in each case; 50,000 deputies and 50,000 strikers would have been well below the mark. It is noteworthy that although the danger of an uprising in the Pittsburgh district was widely advertised no appeal was made for troops, nor was there even any talk of an appeal. The reason was that the Steel Trust had a vast army of its own, officered by its own officials, and it needed no outside help.

Western Pennsylvania is controlled body and soul by the Steel Trust. The whole district has the psychology of a company-owned town. All authority

[97]

centers in the steel industry. From there practically every institution takes its orders. Local governmental agencies are hardly more than public service departments of the Steel Trust. Their officials, city, county, state and federal, obey the mandates of the steel magnates just about as readily and naturally as do the superintendents and mill bosses. No less than the latter they felt it to be their duty to break the strike by whatever means their masters told them to use.

With the approach of the strike these lackey officials hastened *en masse* to the aid of the Steel Trust. Sheriff Haddock, besides swearing in an army of guards and turning them over to the steel companies to carry out their plan of terrorism, issued a flaming proclamation practically setting up martial law and making it a riotous assembly for three steel workers to meet together. Next day, September 21, the organizers tried to hold a meeting in North Clairton — with the Burgess' permission, and at a place on the public commons especially set aside by the authorities for union meetings. About 3,000 steel workers gathered to hear the speakers. Everything was going as peacefully as a Sunday school picnic, when suddenly a troop of State Constabulary appeared upon the scene, and without a word of warning, rode full tilt into the crowd, clubbing and trampling men and women indiscriminately. They tore down and threw in the mud the American flag floating above the speakers' stand. Scores were arrested (including organizers J. B. Etchison and P. H. Brogan) and held for heavy bonds on charges of rioting.[1]   Many were seriously injured, but fearing to report their cases to the doctors and thus court arrest, as the latter were nearly all deputies, they cured themselves as best they could.   This crying outrage was perpetrated under the authority of the Sheriff's proclamation.   It was endorsed and lauded by Governor Sproul, than whom the Steel Trust has no more willing champion.

At the same hour as the Clairton outrage a similar attack was made on the workers at Glassport, adjoining McKeesport.   Not being allowed to meet at the latter city the organizers had leased a plot of ground in Glassport and had been holding regular meetings there, with the full sanction of the local authorities.   For the meeting in question they had an official permit.   But just as it was about to begin the State Constabulary broke it up in true Cossack fashion, almost riding down the Burgess in so doing. They arrested all they could seize.   These were held as rioters under bail of from $1,000 to $3,000 each. The venal Pittsburgh papers screamed about the outbreaks that had been crushed by the gallant State police, and praised them for their bravery in facing the " rioting mobs."

Despite all these terroristic methods the Steel

[1] In this connection occurred one of the finest incidents in the strike: Wm. J. Brennan, an able, conscientious attorney of Pittsburgh, and one of the counsel who defended the Homestead strikers in 1892, went to Clairton to get the " rioters " released on bonds. But such a state of terror existed that no one dared to go their bail. Thereupon, Mr. Brennan himself, without knowing a single one of the defendants, but smarting under the injustice of it all, pledged his entire property holdings, amounting to $88,000, to get them set free.

Trust could not break the will of its workers. On September 22 they struck throughout the entire industry with a discipline and universality that will be remembered so long as steel is made in America. On Tuesday, the twenty-third, 304,000 had quit their posts in the mills and furnaces. All week their ranks were augmented until by September 30, there were 365,600 on strike. It was a magnificent effort for freedom, and twice as big a strike as this country had ever known. By cities and districts, the numbers of strikers were as follows:

Pittsburgh	25,000
Homestead	9,000
Braddock	10,000
Rankin	5,000
Clairton	4,000
Duquesne & McKeesport	12,000
Vandergrift	4,000
Brackenridge	5,000
New Kensington	1,100
Apollo	1,500
Leechburg	3,000
Donora & Monessen	12,000
Johnstown	18,000
Coatesville	4,000
Youngstown district, including Youngstown, E. Youngstown, Struthers, Hubbard, Niles, Canton, Alliance, Massillon, Warren, Farrell, Newcastle, Sharon, Butler, etc.	70,000
Wheeling district	15,000
Cleveland	25,000
Steubenville district	12,000

Chicago district,
  including Gary, Joilet, DeKalb, South
  Chicago, Indiana Harbor, East Chicago,
  Hammond, Evanston, Sterling, Peoria,
  Milwaukee, etc. 90,000
Buffalo district 12,000
Pueblo 6,000
Birmingham 2,000
5 Bethlehem Plants 20,000
                                      ―――――
        Total................365,600

The shutdown was almost complete. Throughout the country the industry was stricken with
paralysis. On an average the strike was at least
90 per cent. effective. In the great Chicago district practically all the men struck, hamstringing the
big plants in the various steel towns of that section,
Gary, Joliet, Indiana Harbor, South Chicago, etc.
The holding of the organizations in this district for
a year, in the face of Steel Trust opposition, by the
organizers under Secretary Evans, and later, De
Young, was one of the most notable achievements of
the whole campaign. When the pent-up force was
finally released it swept the district like a flood,
leaving hardly a wheel turning anywhere.

Youngstown is another place where great difficulties had been encountered in the organizing work,
the workers being deeply discouraged by recently
lost local strikes, and the authorities at some points
so hostile that it was impossible to hold meetings in
the strategic places. But so widespread was the discontent at the miserable working conditions, and so
well had the district crew of organizers under Secre-

taries McCadden and Hammersmark done their work that when the strike clarion sounded, the masses of steel workers responded almost to a man. Trust plants and " independents " alike had to shut down. The steel working population of the entire Mahoning Valley went on holiday. It was a clean walkout. In the outer Youngstown district, as established by the National Committee system, the companies, by the use of desperate tactics, succeeded in keeping some of their men at work; in Sharon, Farrell and Newcastle probably twenty per cent refused to obey the strike call. But in Canton and Massillon, John Olchon and the other organizers brought all the important mills to a dead stop.

Without exception, the enormous Cleveland mills and furnaces shut down tight. In Johnstown the Cambria Company was so hard hit that, swallowing its pride, it had to ask the hated unions for a detachment of workers to protect its plants. The Buffalo district men struck almost 100 per cent., after a bitter organizing campaign and an eight months' free speech fight. The Wheeling and Steubenville districts' steel mills and blast furnaces were abandoned altogether by their crews. In Coatesville and Birmingham, the response was poor, in the first locality because of insufficient organization; and in the second because of discouragement due to a lost local strike the year before. But in far away Colorado, the steel workers, hearkening to the voice of freedom abroad in the land, expressed their contempt for the company-union slavery of John D. Rockefeller, Jr., by tieing up every department in his big Pueblo mills.

In the immediate Pittsburgh district, though here more strenuously opposed by the Steel Trust, the strike ranged from 75 to 85 per cent. effective. That it did not go as strong as other districts was purely because of the denial, by the companies and the authorities, of the workers' rights to meet and to organize. In the " Black Valley " section of the district, comprising the towns lying along the Allegheny river, Apollo, Vandergrift, Leechburg, Brackenbridge, Natrona and New Kensington, and notorious as the scene of the brutal murder of organizer Mrs. Fannie Sellins, the strike went 90 per cent. or better; but in the Monongahela river section it was not so good. Of the steel towns in that district, Donora and Monessen took the lead with a 100 per cent. strike. Due to the terrorism prevailing exact figures were almost impossible to get for the other towns, but according to the best information procurable they averaged about as follows; Clairton 95, Braddock 90, Homestead 80, Rankin 85, McKeesport 70, and Duquesne 50 per cent. In Pittsburgh itself all the larger mills and furnaces, except those of the Jones and Laughlin Company, either suspended operations altogether or lost heavily of their employees during the first two days of the strike. The Jones and Laughlin men had been profoundly discouraged by a lost strike two years previously, and had responded poorly to the organizers' efforts. But when they saw the magnitude of the strike they took heart somewhat, and by strenuous efforts in a rapid fire campaign, the organizers had at least 60 per cent. of them on strike by the end of the first week.

In the plants of the Bethlehem Steel Company

the strike did not become effective until September 29. The cause was to be found in local conditions. In the early spring of 1918, before the National Committee began its campaign, ruthless exploitation by the company had resulted in a strike of machine shop employees. The National War Labor Board settled the strike, erecting a shop organization to handle grievances. In the meantime the National Committee came into the field and began active operations. Up till this time the organized movement, led by David Williams and Patrick Duffy, had been confined principally to the Machinists, Electrical workers and a few other skilled trades; but now it spread to the main body of the employees. To head it off the company proposed to the National Committee that a Rockefeller union be set up in the plants. Naturally this was unacceptable. Then they offered to sign an agreement covering all their shipyard employees if the organization of their steel plants was given up, feeling no doubt that the shipyard boom was only temporary. For the National Committee, John Fitzpatrick spurned this shameful trade, and the organization campaign went on — with the shipyard men getting their agreement later on just the same.

Technically the employees of the Bethlehem Company should have struck under the first strike call, as they had no union agreement; but being tied up with futile negotiations under their " collective bargaining " arrangement, they did not get out until the twenty-ninth. When they did strike the response was not so good. A fair average for the plants in South Bethlehem, Steelton, Reading, Lebanon and

Sparrows' Point would be a 50 per cent. strike.

On the whole the strike affected practically the entire industry, seventy important steel centres being involved. About the only mills of consequence to escape it were those located at Midland, Woodlawn, Lorain and Duluth. And the only reason for this was lack of sufficient organizers to cover them. It is noteworthy that the strike followed strictly the lines of organization. In hardly a single instance did the unorganized go out spontaneously, even though they had previously been clamoring for the unions to help them. This tends to show how completely the steel companies dominated their unorganized workers and how hard it was for the latter to act in concert.

For the most part the great walkout was concentrated on the smelting and rolling branches of the steel industry. It had been the original intention to make the movement thoroughly industrial, taking in all the workers from those who mine the coal and iron to those who transfer the finished products to the railroad lines. But insufficient resources compelled the modification of this program, and forced the unions to confine their work principally to the blast furnaces and rolling mills. However, where the company mines or fabricating works lay close to the general plants, or were part of them, the essentially industrial character of the campaign manifested itself and these departments were organized along with the rest. In various places, including Gary, Chicago, Homestead, etc., bridge, car, and other fabricating shops were an integral part of the drive. The iron miners working close in to Birm-

[105]

ingham responded to some extent, but a big defeat of the local metal trades in the mills a couple of years previously held them back from making a strong demonstration. The coal miners struck in several places. In Johnstown, 2,000 of them working in the Cambria Steel Company's mines organized during the campaign, became affiliated with the local mill workers' council, and walked out 100 per cent. on the historic twenty-second of September.

Although the United States Steel Corporation was recognized as the arch enemy of the unions, the strike was not directed against it alone. Every iron and steel mill and furnace in the country not working under union agreements was included. This meant at least 95 per cent. of the industry, because the only agreements of any consequence were between some of the smaller companies and the Amalgamated Association. A number of these concerns were affected also, their agreements relating only to skilled workers, and the plants having to close when the laborers struck. This occurred quite extensively in the Cleveland, Youngstown and Pittsburgh districts.

Considering the large number of them involved and their traditions of isolated action, the unions displayed reasonably good solidarity in going " over the top " against the Steel Trust. The battle line was far from perfect, however. Much harm was done the morale of the strikers by local unions here and there that were under the sway of ignorant blockheads or designing tools of the bosses, refusing to recognize the National Committee's strike call and insisting upon getting instructions from their own headquarters, meanwhile scabbing it in the mills. And the worst of it was that sometimes it was difficult, or even impossible to have the necessary instructions issued.

Far more serious than this, however, was the action of the executive officers of the International Union of Steam and Operating Engineers. Just as the strike was about to begin President Snellings and Secretary Comerford sharply condemned it by letter and through the press, urging their men to stay at work upon the flimsy pretext that the President's industrial conference would attend to their interests. Roused to indignation by this cold-blooded course, the local unions of engineers, almost without exception, repudiated their international misleaders and struck with the rest of the steel workers. After President Gompers had been quoted in the newspapers as pledging the support of the A. F. of L. to the strike (two days after it started) and Labor generally had shown its determination to stick by the steel workers, the officers of the Engineers' international were compelled to publicly endorse the strike. But throughout its duration they nevertheless privately encouraged their strategically situated tradesmen to return to work, thus doing incalculable harm when the strikers had begun to weaken a little. This plain case of official scabbery was inspired by a jurisdictional dispute between the engineers and the electrical workers over the disposition to be made of electrical cranemen signed up in the campaign. Because they could not have their unreasonable way in the matter, the officials of the engineers deliberately knifed the strike and lent aid and comfort to the bitterest opponents of Organized Labor on this planet. To such extremes will union men go in internecine wars over trade demarcations.

But in spite of opposition, blundering and treachery, the steel workers had spoken. Mr. Gary was answered. Previous to the strike, he declared that the unions represented only an insignificant minority of his men, the great bulk of his working force being satisfied. He compelled the Committee to show its credentials. Result: 365,600 steel workers laid down their tools. This estimated total has never been disputed by the steel companies. Here and there, in some individual town or district, they pointed out a figure occasionally as being excessive; but although importuned by newspaper men to do so, they never ventured to issue a statement of the number on strike at all points. The reason was that they feared to print the grand total which even their lying press bureau would have to admit. Word came to the Committee from reliable sources that the steel manufacturers considered the union figure well within the real total.

While not accurately ascertainable, the number of Mr. Gary's employees actually taking part in the strike may be closely approximated. Mr. Gary stated to the Senate Committee that the total number employed by the United States Steel Corporation in the departments affected by the strike was 201,065. Against this number should be checked off about half of the total number of strikers, or 182,500. This is based upon the theory that the official U. S. Steel Corporation plants form approximately 50 per cent. of the industry, and that the strike was just as effective against them as against those of any other company. It is not asserted that these figures are absolutely accurate; but they will serve to indicate that the claim of a 90 per cent. strike in the plants of the Steel Corporation is a fair one. It is exceedingly doubtful if as many as 10 per cent. of Mr. Gary's employees remained at their posts and failed to heed the strike call. Fully 125,-000 of them were members of the unions before the strike started, and most of the rest would have been also, had they dared brave the anger of their bosses.

The great steel strike thoroughly exposed the hypocrisies of Mr. Gary and his ilk that in some mysterious way labor policies and conditions in the steel industry depend upon the wishes of the body of the workers. It made plain that in the autocratic system now prevailing the democratic principles of majority and minority do not enter. It is a case pure and simple of the absolute sway of property rights over human rights. A handful of social parasites hidden away in Wall street, with no other interest in the steel industry than to exploit it, settle arbitrarily the vital questions of wages, hours and working conditions, while the enormous mass of the workers, actual producers whose very lives are involved, have no say whatsoever. No matter how bitter their grievances, when they raise their voice to ask redress, they are discharged, blacklisted, starved, beaten, jailed and even shot, until they bend the knee again and yield to the will of their industrial masters.

VIII

GARYISM RAMPANT

THE WHITE TERROR — CONSTITUTIONAL RIGHTS
DENIED — UNBREAKABLE SOLIDARITY — FATHER
KAZINCY — THE COSSACKS — SCIENTIFIC BAR-
BARITY — PROSTITUTED COURTS — SERVANTS RE-
WARDED

IT was the misfortune of the steel strike to occur in
the midst of the post-war reaction, which still persists
unabated, and which constitutes the most shameful
page in American history. Ours are days when the
organized employers, inspired by a horrible fear of
the onward sweep of revolution in Europe and the
irresistible advance of the labor movement in this
country, are robbing the people over-night of their
most precious rights, the fruits of a thousand years
of struggle. And the people, not yet recovered
from war hysteria and misled by a corrupt press, cannot perceive the outrage. They even glory in their
degradation. Free speech, free press, free assembly, as we once knew these rights, are now things
of the past. What poor rudiments of them remain depend upon the whims of a Burleson, or
the rowdy element of the American Legion. Hundreds of idealists, guilty of nothing more than
a temperate expression of their honest views, lan-
guish in prison serving sentences so atrocious as to

shock the world — although Europe has long since released its war and political prisoners. Working class newspapers are raided, denied the use of the mails and suppressed. Meetings are broken up by Chamber of Commerce mobs or thugs in public office. The right of asylum is gone — the infamous Palmer is deporting hundreds who dare to hold views different from his. The right of the workers to organize is being systematically curtailed; and crowning shame of all, workingmen can no longer have legislative representatives of their own choosing. In a word, America, from being the most forward-looking, liberty-loving country in the world, has in two short years become one of the most reactionary. We in this country are patiently enduring tyranny that would not be tolerated in England, France, Italy, Russia or Germany. Our great war leaders promised us the New Freedom; they have given us the White Terror.

Realizing full well the reactionary spirit of the times, the steel companies proceeded safely to extremes to crush the steel strike, dubbed by them an attempt at violent revolution. To accomplish their end they stuck at nothing. One of their most persistent and determined efforts was to deprive the steel workers of their supposedly inalienable right to meet and talk together. Throughout the strike, whenever and wherever they could find municipal or court officials willing to do their bidding, the steel barons abolished the rights of free speech and free assembly, so precious to strikers. Few districts escaped this evil, but as usual, Pennsylvania felt the blow earliest and heaviest. Hardly had the strike started when the oily Schwab prohibited meetings in Bethlehem; the Allegheny and West Penn Steel Companies did the same at Natrona, jailing organizer J. McCaig for " inciting to riot "; in the Sharon-Farrell district the steel workers, denied their constitutional rights in their home towns, had to march several miles over into Ohio (America they called it) in order to hold their meetings.

Along the Monongahela river the shut-down was complete. Following Sheriff Haddock's proclamation and the " riots " at Clairton and Glassport, it was only a few days until the city and borough officials had completely banned strike meetings in all the territory from Charleroi to Pittsburgh. The unions' free-speech, free-assembly victory of the past summer was instantly cancelled. For forty-one miles through the heart of America's steel industry, including the important centers of Monessen, Donora, Clairton, Wilson, Glassport, McKeesport, Duquesne, Homestead, Braddock, Rankin, etc., not a meeting of the steel workers could be held. Even in Pittsburgh itself meetings were prohibited everywhere except in Labor Temple. The steel-collared city officials never could quite muster the gall to close Labor's own building — or perhaps because it is so far from the mills and so poorly situated for meetings they felt it to be of no use to the strikers. Thus the Steel Trust gave its workers a practical demonstration of what is meant by the phrase, " making the world safe for democracy."

Not only were mass meetings forbidden, but so also were regular business meetings under the charters of the local unions. To test out this particular usurpation, Attorney W. H. Rubin, then in charge of the strike's legal department and possessed of a keener faith in Pennsylvania justice than the Strike committee had, keener probably than he himself now has, prayed the Allegheny County Court of Common Pleas to enjoin Mayor Babcock and other city officials from interfering with a local union of the Amalgamated Association holding its business meetings on the south side of the city where its members lived and where several large mills are located. At the hearing the Mayor and Chief of Police freely admitted that there had been no violence in the strike, and even complimented the men on their behavior, but they feared there might be trouble and so forbade the meetings. The honorable Judges Ford and Shafer agreed with them and denied the writ, saying among other things:

> It is the duty of the Mayor and Police Department to preserve the peace, and it must be sometimes necessary for that purpose to prevent the congregating in one place of large numbers of people such as might get beyond the control of the Police Department, and it must be left to the reasonable discretion of the officers charged with keeping the peace when such intervention is made.

In other words, the sacred right of the workers to meet together depends upon the arbitrary will of any politician who may get into the office controlling the permits. Shortly before Judges Ford and Shafer handed down this noble conception of free assembly, Judge Kennedy of the Allegheny County Court, ruling on the appeal of Mother Jones, J. L. Beaghen, J. M. Patterson and Wm. Z.

[113]

Foster in the Duquesne free speech cases of several weeks prior to the strike, had this to say:

> It cannot be questioned that the object of these meetings — increasing the membership in the American Federation of Labor — is a perfectly lawful one, but the location of the meetings in the Monongahela valley, built up as it is for mile after mile of an unbroken succession of iron and steel mills, and thickly populated with iron workers, many of whom obviously are not members of this association, and among whom, on both sides, there are, in all probability, some who upon the occasion of meetings such as these purported to be, might through excitement precipitate serious actions of which the consequences could not be foreseen and might be disastrous, presents questions which are sufficient to cause the court to hesitate before interfering with the exercise of discretion on the part of the Mayor in refusing to permit such meetings at this time.

The Court is still hesitating to interfere with Mayor Crawford's tyranny, and the defendants had to pay $100 and costs each for trying to hold a meeting on ground they had leased. One would think that the remedy in the case conjured out of thin air by the learned judge (for in the thousands of meetings held in the steel campaign he cannot point to one incident of violence) would be for the local authorities to provide ample police protection to insure order. But no, in Pennsylvania the thing to do is to set aside the constitutional rights of the workers. Would such action be taken in the case of members of a Chamber of commerce? Wouldn't the governor, rather, order out the state troops, if necessary, to uphold their right of assembly?

[114]

In the hope of getting some relief, or at the least some publicity about the unbearable situation, a committee of 18 local labor men, representing the largest trade unions in Western Pennsylvania, went to Washington and presented to the Allegheny County congressional delegation a petition expressing contempt for the judges and other officials in their part of the State and asking Congress to give them the justice these men refused to mete out. Surely, the Allegheny County congressmen were exactly the ones to bring the Steel Trust to time. With a grand flourish they introduced a resolution into the House calling for an investigation — then they forgot all about it.

The official tyranny and outlawry along the Monongahela was so bad that the Pennsylvania Federation of Labor had to voice its protest. On November 1–2 it held a special convention in Pittsburgh, attended by several hundred delegates. A resolution was adopted demanding that protection be given the rights of the workers, and that if the authorities failed to extend this protection, " the Executive Council of the Pennsylvania Federation of Labor shall issue a call for a State-wide strike, when in its judgment it is necessary to compel respect for law and the restoration of liberty as guaranteed by the Constitution of the United States and of the State of Pennsylvania." For this action President Jas. H. Maurer of the Federation was hotly assailed and even menaced with lynching by the lawless business interests.

By some inexplicable mental twist the ex-union man Burgess of Homestead eventually allowed the

[115]

unions to hold one mass meeting each week — to this day the only ones permitted in the forty-one miles of Monongahela steel towns. They were under the supervision of the State police. At each meeting a half dozen of these Cossacks, in full uniform, would sit upon the platform as censors. Only English could be spoken. As the saying was, all the organizers were permitted to talk about was the weather. When one touched on a vital strike phase a Cossack would yell at him, " Hey, cut that out! You're through, you — ! Don't ever come back here any more." And he never could speak there again.

Judging from past experiences the strike in the Pittsburgh district should have been impossible under such hard circumstances. With little or no opportunity to meet for mutual encouragement and enlightenment, the strikers, theoretically, should have been soon discouraged and driven back to work. But they were saved by their matchless solidarity, bred of a deep faith in the justice of their cause. In the black, Cossack-ridden Monongahela towns there were thousands of strikers who were virtually isolated, who never attended a meeting during the entire strike and seldom if ever saw an organizer or read a strike bulletin, yet they fought on· doggedly for three and one-half months, buoyed up by a boundless belief in the ultimate success of their supreme effort. Each felt himself bound to stay away from the mills, come weal or come woe, regardless of what the rest did. These were mainly the despised foreigners, of course, but their splendid fighting qualities were a never-ending revelation and inspiration to all connected with the strike.

Through the dark night of oppression a bright beacon of liberty gleamed from Braddock. There the heroic Slavish priest, Reverend Adelbert Kazincy, pastor of St. Michel's Roman Catholic church, bade defiance to the Steel Trust and all its minions. He threw open his church to the strikers, turned his services into strike meetings, and left nothing undone to make the men hold fast. The striking steel workers came to his church from miles around, Protestants as well as Catholics. The neighboring clergymen who ventured to oppose the strike lost their congregations,— men, women and children flocked to Father Kazincy's, and all of them stood together, as solid as a brick wall.

Reverend Kazincy's attitude aroused the bitterest hostility of the steel companies. They did not dare to do him bodily violence, nor to close his church by their customary "legal" methods; but they tried everything else. Unable to get the local bishop to silence him, they threatened finally to strangle his church. To this the doughty priest replied that if they succeeded he would put a monster sign high up on his steeple: "This church destroyed by the Steel Trust," and he would see that it stayed there. When they tried to foreclose on the church mortgage, he promptly laid the matter before his heterogeneous congregation of strikers, who raised the necessary $1200 before leaving the building and next day brought in several hundred dollars more. Then the companies informed him that after the strike no more Slovaks could get work in the mills. He told them that if they tried this, he would do his level best to pull all the Slovaks out of the district (they are the bulk of the mill forces) and colonize them in the West. The promised blacklist has not yet materialized.

Father Kazincy and the clergymen who worked with him, notable among whom was the Reverend Molnar, a local Slavish Lutheran minister, consti- tuted one of the great mainstays of the strike in their district. They are men who have caught the true spirit of the lowly Nazarene. The memory of their loyal co-operation will long live green in the hearts of the Pittsburgh district steel strikers.

A description of the repressive measures taken by the Steel Trust against its workers during the early period of the strikes necessarily relates almost entirely to Western Pennsylvania. With few ex- ceptions, the other districts were in a deadlock. So tightly were the mills shut down that the companies could hardly stir. It took them several weeks to get their stricken fighting machinery in motion again. But it was different in Western Pennsylvania, in what we call the greater Pittsburgh district; that has always been the key to the whole industry, and there, from the very first, the steel companies made a bit- ter fight to control the situation and to break the strike. The tactics used there are typical in that they came to be universally applied as the strike grew older, the degree of their application depending upon the amount of control exercised by the Steel Trust in the several localities.

To carry on the terror so well begun by the suppression of free speech and free assembly, the Steel Trust turned loose upon the devoted strikers in Western Pennsylvania the great masses of armed thugs it had been recruiting since long before the strike. These consisted of every imaginable type of armed guard, official and unofficial, except uniformed troops. There were State Constabulary, deputy sheriffs, city police, city detectives, company police, company detectives, private detectives, coal and iron police, ordinary gunmen, armed strike-breakers, vigilantes, and God knows how many others. These legions of reaction, all tarred with the same brush — a servile, mercenary allegiance to the ruthless program of the Steel Trust — vied with each other in working hardships upon the steel workers. In this shameful competition the State Constabulary stood first; for downright villainy and disregard of civil and human rights, these so-called upholders of law and order easily outdistanced all the other plug-uglies assembled by the Steel Trust. They merit our special attention.

The Pennsylvania State Constabulary dates from 1905, when a law was enacted creating the Department of State Police. The force is modelled somewhat along the lines of the Royal Irish Constabulary and the Canadian Northwest Mounted Police. The men are uniformed, mounted, heavily armed and regularly enlisted. For the most part they consist of ex-United States army men. At present they number somewhat less than the amount set by law, 415 officers and men. Their ostensible duty is to patrol the poorly policed rural sections of the state, and this they do when they have nothing else to take up their time.   But their real function is to break strikes.   They were organized as a result of the failure of the militia to crush the anthracite strike of 1902.   Since their inception they have taken an active part in all important industrial disturbances within their jurisdiction.   They are the heart's darlings of Pennsylvania's great corporations. Labor regards them with an abiding hatred.   Says Mr. Jas. H. Maurer (*The Cossack*, page 3) :

> The " English Square " is the only open-field military formation of human beings that has ever been known to repulse cavalry.   All other formations go down before the resistless rush of plunging beasts mounted by armed men, mad in the fierce excitement induced by the thundering gallop of charging horses. A charge by cavalry is a storm from hell — for men on foot.   A cavalry-man's power, courage and daring are strangely multiplied by the knowledge that he sits astride a swift, strong beast, willing and able to knock down a dozen men in one leap of this terrible rush. Hence, the Cossacks, the mounted militiamen — for crushing unarmed, unmounted groups of men on strike.

But the State Police do not confine themselves merely to the crude business of breaking up so-called strike riots.   Their forte is prevention, rather than cure.   They aim to so terrorize the people that they will cower in their homes, afraid to go upon the streets to transact necessary business, much less to congregate in crowds.   They play unmercifully upon every fear and human weakness.   They are skilled, scientific terrorists, such as Czarist Russia never had.

On a thousand occasions they beat, shot, jailed or trampled steel workers under their horses' hoofs in the manner and under the circumstances best calculated to strike terror to their hearts. In Braddock, for instance, a striker having died of natural causes, about two hundred of his fellows assembled to accompany the body to the cemetery. To stop this harmless demonstration all the State Police needed to do was to send a word to the union. But such orderly, reasonable methods do not serve their studied policy of frightfulness. Therefore, without previously informing the strikers in any way that their funeral party was obnoxious, the Cossacks laid in wait for the procession, and when it reached the heart of town, where all Braddock could get the benefit of the lesson in "Americanism," they swooped down upon it at full gallop, clubbing the participants and scattering them to the four winds.

Similar outrageous attacks occurred not once, but dozens of times. Let Father Kazincy speak of his experiences:

Braddock, Pa., Sept. 27, 1919

W. Z. Foster,
   Pittsburgh, Pa.,
Dear Sir:

The pyramidal impudence of the State Constabulary in denying charges of brutal assaults perpetrated by them upon the peaceful citizens of the borough of Braddock prompts me to send a telegram to the Governor of Pennsylvania, in which I have offered to bring forth two specific cases of bestial transgression of their " calling."

On Monday last at 10 A. M. my congregation, leaving church, was suddenly, without any cause whatever,

[121]

attacked on the very steps of the Temple of God, by the Constables, and dispersed by the iron-hoofed Huns. Whilst dispersing indignation and a blood frenzy swayed them, a frenzy augmented by that invisible magnetic force, the murmuring, raging force of 3,000 strong men. One could feel that helpless feeling of being lifted up by some invisible force, forced, thrown against the flux of raging, elemental passion of resentment, against the Kozaks of this State.

Nevertheless, it was the most magnificent display of self-control manifested by the attacked ever shown anywhere. They moved on, with heads lowered and jaws firmly set, to submit. Oh, it was great; it was magnificent. They, these husky, muscle-bound Titans of raw force walked home . . . only thinking, thinking hard. Oh, only for one wink from some one, would there be a puddle of red horseblood mixed with the human kind.

But no. We want to win the strike. We want to win the confidence of the public.

Tuesday afternoon the little babies of No. 1 were going to the school. They loitered for the school bell to summon them. And here come Kozaks. They see the little innocents standing on the steps of the schoolhouse, their parents on the opposite side of the street. What a splendid occasion to start the " Hunkey's " ire. Let us charge their babies — that will fetch them to an attack upon us.

They did. But the " Hunkey " even at the supreme test of his cool-headedness, refused to flash his knife to save his babies from the onrush of the cruel horses' hoofs.

I am relating to you, Mr. Foster, things as they happened. You may use my name in connection with your charges against the Constabulary.

Sincerely yours, REV. A. KAZINCY,
416 Frazier St., Braddock, Pa.

COSSACKS IN ACTION

Brutal and unprovoked assault upon Rudolph Dressel, Homestead, Pa., Sept. 23, 1919.

Photo by International

Governor Sproul paid no attention to Father Kazincy's protest, nor did he to a long letter from Jas. H. Maurer, reciting shocking brutalities fully authenticated by affidavits — unless it was to multiply his public endorsements and praises of the State Police.

A favorite method of the Constables was to go tearing through the streets (foreign quarter), forcing pedestrians into whatever houses they happened to be passing, regardless of whether or not they lived there. Read these two typical affidavits, portraying a double outrage:

STATE OF PENNSYLVANIA⎱
COUNTY OF ALLEGHENY⎰ ss.

Before me, the undersigned authority, personally appeared John Bodnar, who being duly sworn according to law deposes and says that he lives at 542 Gold Way, Homestead, Pa., that on Tuesday, Sept. 23, 1919, at about 2 P. M. he went to visit his cousin on Fifth Avenue, Homestead, Pa.: that he did in fact visit his cousin and after leaving the house of his cousin was accosted on the street by a member of the State Police who commanded him, the deponent, to enter a certain house, which house was not known to the deponent; that deponent informed said State Policeman that he, deponent, did not live in the house indicated by the State Policeman; nevertheless, the said State Policeman said, " It makes no difference whether you live in there or not, you go in there anyhow "; thereupon in fear of violence deponent did enter the said house, which house was two doors away from the house of the cousin of deponent; that after a time deponent came out of the house into which he had been ordered, thereupon the

[123]

same State Policeman returned and ordered deponent to re-enter the house aforesaid and upon again being informed by deponent that he, the deponent, did not live in said house, the said State Policeman forthwith arrested the deponent and brought him to Homestead police station, and at a hearing at said station before the burgess was fined the sum of nine dollars and sixty-five cents, which amount was paid by deponent.

JOHN BODNAR

Sworn to and subscribed before me
this first day of October, 1919.
A. F. Kaufman, Notary Public.

Here is what happened in the house into which Bodnar was driven:

STATE OF PENNSYLVANIA ⎱
COUNTY OF ALLEGHENY ⎰ ss.

Before me, the undersigned authority, personally appeared Steve Dudash, who being duly sworn according to law deposes and says that he resides at 541 E. 5th Ave., Homestead, Pa.; that on Tuesday September 23, 1919, in the afternoon of said day, his wife, Mary Dudash, was severely scalded, burned, and injured by reason of a sudden fright sustained when a State Policeman forced John Bodnar into the home of the deponent and his wife, Mary Dudash; that said Mary Dudash, the wife of the deponent, was in a very delicate condition at the time of the fright and injury complained of, caused by the State Police and that on Sunday, Sept. 28, 1919, following the date in question, namely the 23rd, the said Mary Dudash, wife of deponent, gave birth to a child; that on account of the action of the State Police in forcing John Bodnar with terror into the home of deponent and his wife, Mary

Dudash, she, the said Mary Dudash, wife of the de-
pondent, has been rendered very sick and has suffered
a nervous collapse and is still suffering from the nervous shock sustained, on account of the action of the
State Police, above referred to.

STEVE DUDASH

Sworn to and subscribed before me
this first day of October, 1919
A. F. Kaufman, Notary Public

When on a mission of terrorism the first thing
the State Troopers do is to get their horses onto
the sidewalks, the better to ride down the pedestrians. Unbelievable though it may seem, they actually ride into stores and inner rooms. Picture the
horror a foreign worker and his family, already
badly frightened, at seeing a mounted policeman
crashing into their kitchen. The horses are highly
trained. Said an N. E. A. news dispatch, Sept.
26th, 1919:

> Horses of the Pennsylvania State Constabulary are
> trained not to turn aside, as a horse naturally will do,
> when a person stands in its way, but to ride straight
> over any one against whom they are directed. Lizzie,
> a splendid black mare ridden by Trooper John A.
> Thorp, on duty at Homestead, uses her teeth as well
> as her heels when in action. Her master will some-
> times dismount, leaving Lizzie to hold a striker with
> her strong jaws, while he takes up the pursuit of others
> on foot.

If this is thought to be an overdrawn statement,
read the following affidavit:

[125]

Butler, Pa., October 3, 1919

I, Jacob Sazuta,
   21 Bessemer Ave.,
    Lyndora, Pa.

Commenced work for the Standard Steel Car Company in September, 1913, as laborer. About October 1916 was promoted to car fitter in the erection department; in February, 1919, was then taken and placed as a wheel roller, and I worked in this capacity until August 6th, 1919 [the date the steel strike began there].

On August 25, after receiving my pay, I was standing looking in a store window, when State Trooper No. 52 rode his horse upon me, THE HORSE STEPPING ON MY LEFT FOOT. Trooper No. 52 ordered me to move on, BUT AS THE HORSE WAS STANDING ON MY FOOT I COULD NOT MOVE. He then struck me across the head with his club, cutting a gash in the left side of my head that took the doctor three stitches to close up the wound. After hitting me with his club, he kept chasing me with his horse.

JACOB SAZUTA

Sworn and subscribed before me
this third day of October, 1919.
   E. L. Cefferi, Notary Public.

A few affidavits, and extracts from affidavits, taken at random from among the hundreds in possession of the National Committee, will indicate the general conditions prevailing in the several districts:

Clairton, Pa.

John Doban, Andy Niski and Mike Hudak were walking home along the street when the State Police came and arrested the three, making ten holes in Mike

[126]

Hudak's head.　Were under arrest three days.　Union bailed them out, $1,000.00 each.

Butler, Pa., Oct. 3, 1919.

I, James Torok,
　Storekeeper,
　　103 Standard Ave.,
　　　Lyndora, Pa.,

On about August 15, 1919, I saw State Troopers chase a crippled man who could not run as fast as his horse, and run him down, the horse bumping him in the back with his head, knocked him down.　Later three men were coming to my store to buy some things; the State Troopers ran their horses right on them and chased them home.　One of the men stopped and said: "I have to go to the store," and the Trooper said: "Get to hell out of here, you sons — ——, or I will kill you," and started after them again, and the people ran home and stayed away from the store.

JAMES TOROK

Sworn to and subscribed before me this
3rd day of October, 1919.
　E. L. Peffer, Notary Public.

Homestead, Pa.

. . . two State Policemen made a forcible entry into the home of deponent, Trachn Yenchenke, at 327 Third Ave, Homestead, Pa., and came to the place where deponent was asleep, kicked him and punched him, and handled him with extreme violence and took deponent without any explanation, without permitting deponent to dress, dragged him half naked from his home to waiting automobile and conveyed him against his will to the Homestead Police Station. . . .　Fined $15.10.

TRACHN YENCHENKE.

Monessen, Pa.

. . . Concetta Cocchiara, 8 months advanced in a state of pregnancy, was out shopping with her sister. Two State Policemen brusquely ordered them home and when they did not move fast enough to suit, followed them home, forced himself into the house and struck affiant with a stick on the head and grabbed her by the hair and pulled her from the kitchen and forced her into a patrol wagon and took her to the borough jail, . . . Sworn to before Henry Fusarini, Notary Public, October 11, 1919.

———————

Newcastle, Pa.

John Simpel,
    1711 Morris Ave.,
        Newcastle.

On Sept. 22, about 5.30 P. M. he was walking along towards his home on Moravia Street. Hearing shots fired he stopped in the middle of the street and was instantly struck by bullets three times, one bullet going through his leg, one through his finger, while the third entered his back and went through his body, coming out through his abdomen. The shots were fired from inside the gates of the Carnegie Steel Company's plant. Mr. Simpel believes the shots were fired from a machine gun, because of their rapid succession. He fell on the ground and lay there for about ten minutes, until he was picked up by a young boy. . . . He is now totally disabled. He has a wife and a child and is 48 years of age. . . .

JAS. A. NORRINGTON, Secretary.

———————

Farrell, Pa.

. . . There were four men killed here, one in a quarrel in a boarding house and three by the Cossacks. Half a dozen were wounded, one of them a woman. She

[128]

was shot in the back by a Cossack, while on her way to the butcher shop. . . .

S. COATES, Secretary.

Many hundreds of similar cases could be cited. In the steel strike a score were killed, almost all on the workers' side; hundreds were seriously injured, and thousands unjustly jailed. To the State Constabulary attaches the blame for a large share of this tyranny. The effect of their activities was to create a condition in Western Pennsylvania, bordering on a reign of terror. Yet it is extremely difficult to definitely fasten their crimes upon them. No matter how dastardly the outrage, when the Steel Trust cracks its whip the local authorities and leading citizens come forth with a mass of affidavits, "white-washing" the thuggery in question, and usually sufficing to cast serious doubts on the statements of the few worker witnesses courageous enough to raise their voices. What is to be thought of the following incident?

Testifying before the Senate Committee investigating the strike, Mr. Gompers related how, in an organizing campaign in Monessen, Pa. several years ago, A. F. of L. organizer Jefferson D. Pierce was bludgeoned by Steel Trust thugs, receiving injuries that resulted in his death. Mr. Gompers had his facts straight. Yet the very next day, Mr. Gary, testifying before the same Committee, produced a sworn statement from the son of Mr. Pierce containing the following assertions:

I was with my father the night he received his injuries in Monessen, Pa., and wish to state very emphatically that his injury was not caused by any one connected with the United States Steel Corporation. On the contrary, it was caused by a member of the I. W. W. organization from out of town, who was sent there at the time to create trouble, as the I. W. W. organization was then trying to gain control of the organizing situation. I wish again most emphatically to refute Mr. Gompers' statement that this injury was caused by some one connected with the United States Steel Corporation.

Upon being questioned, Mr. Gary " thought " that Mr. Pierce is employed at Worcester, Mass. by the American Steel and Wire Company, a subsidiary of the U. S. Steel Corporation.

Fortunately, however, in the steel strike the photographer secured a proof of State Police brutality which the most skilled Steel Trust apologists cannot explain away — a picture of the typically vicious assault upon Mr. R. Dressel, a hotel keeper of 532 Dickson St. (foreign quarter), Homestead, Pa. I quote from the latter's statement in connection therewith:

I, Rudolph Dressel, of the aforesaid address, do hereby make this statement of my own volition and without solicitation from any one. That on the 23rd day of September I was standing in front of my place of business at the aforesaid address and a friend of mine, namely, Adolph Kuehnemund, came to visit and consult me regarding personal matters. As I stood as shown in the picture above mentioned with my friend, the State Constabulary on duty in Homestead came down Dickson St. They had occasion to ride up and down the street several times and finally stopped directly in front of me and demanded that I move on. Before I had time to comply I was struck by the State Policeman. (The attitude of said Policeman is plainly shown in the aforesaid picture, and his threatening club is plainly seen descending towards me.)

My friend and I then entered my place of business and my friend a few minutes afterwards looked out on the street over the summer doors. The policeman immediately charged him and being unable to enter my place of business on horseback, dismounted and entered into my place of business on foot.

My friend being frightened at what had happened to me retired to a room in the rear of my place of business. The Policeman entered this room, accompanied by another State Police, and without cause, reason or excuse, struck my friend and immediately thereafter arrested him. I was personally present at his hearing before Burgess P. H. McGuire of the above city, at which none of the aforesaid policemen were heard or even present. Burgess asked my friend what he was arrested for, and my friend referred to me inasmuch as he himself did not know. The Burgess immediately replied, " We have no time to hear your witnesses," and thereupon levied a fine of $10.00 and costs upon him. My friend having posted a forfeit of $25.00, the sum of $15.45 was deducted therefrom.

The State Constabulary were sent, unasked for, into the quiet steel towns for the sole purpose of intimidating the strikers. The following took place at the meeting of the Braddock Borough Council, October 6:

Mr. Verosky: (County detective and council member) " Mr. Chairman, the citizens of the borough wish to know by whose authority the State Constabulary was called into Braddock to take up their quarters here and to practically relieve the police of their duties, by patrolling the streets on foot, mounted, and always under arms."

Mr. Holtzman: (President of Council) " I surely do not know who called them into town, but were I the Burgess, I would make it my business to find out, in view of the fact that the Constabulary is neither wanted nor needed here."

Mr. Verosky: " Well, in that case, the Burgess may throw some light on the subject."

Mr. Callahan: (Burgess) " The question comes to me as a surprise and I am sure that I don't know by whose authority the Constabulary was called in."

Everything was calm in Braddock until the State Police came in. Then the trouble began. It was the same nearly everywhere. The arrival of these men was always the signal for so-called riots, and wholesale clubbing, shooting and jailing of strikers.

Great praise has been poured upon the State Constabulary for their supposedly wonderful bravery and efficiency, because a few hundred of them, scattered thinly through a score of towns, have been able apparently to overawe many thousands of strikers. But the credit is undeserved. In strikes they always form, in point of actual weight, an insignificant part of the armed forces arrayed against the strikers. For instance, in a steel town, during the strike, there would usually be a dozen or so State Police and from 3,000 to 4,000 deputy sheriffs, company police, etc. The latter classes of gunmen make up the body of the real repressive force; the State Police are merely raiders. It is their particularly dirty job to harass the enemy; to break the strike by scientifically bulldozing the strikers in their homes and on the streets. Thus they are thrown into the limelight, while the company thugs remain in comparative obscurity.

The State Police feel reasonably sure of their skins when carrying on their calculated campaigns of terrorism, for behind them are large numbers of armed guards of various sorts ready to spring to their support at an instant's notice, should the workers dare to resist them. Besides, they know they have *carte blanche* to commit the greatest excesses, since the highest state officials, not to speak of local courts and other authorities, give them undivided support. They are above the law, when the rights of the workers are concerned. Moreover, they realize fully that they can depend upon trade-union leaders to hold the strikers in check from adopting measures of retaliation. Few of them are hurt during their depredations. Once in a while, however, they drive their victims to desperation and get themselves into trouble.

For example, a few days after a fight in Farrell, Pa., that cost the strikers two dead and a dozen seriously wounded, the local secretary there, S. Coates, was on his way to Ohio to hold a meeting, when the delivery truck upon which he was riding overturned, rendering him unconscious. He woke up in a Sharon hospital. The six beds adjoining his were occupied by Cossacks, injured in the riot started by themselves in Farrell. The public knew nothing of their injuries, it being the regular thing to suppress such facts, in order to surround the dreaded Cossacks with a reputation for invulnerability. The way the latter " get even " for their casualties is to victimize and outrage as many workers as they think necessary to balance the score. But such methods cannot go on indefinitely. It will be marvellous, indeed, if some day the State Constabulary, with their policy of deliberate intimidation, are not the means of causing riots such as this country has not yet experienced in labor disputes. Not always will the unions be able to hold their men as steady in the face of brutal provocation as they did in the recent steel strike.

Hand in glove with the Cossacks in their work of terrorizing Pennsylvania's steel towns went the less skilful but equally vicious company police, gunmen, deputy sheriffs, etc., many of whom, ex-service men, disgraced their uniforms by wearing them on strike duty. Nor were the city police, save for a few honorable exceptions here and there, appreciably better. As for the police magistrates, almost to a man they seconded unquestioningly the work of the sluggers. In fact, all the forces of " law and order " in western Pennsylvania, official and unofficial, worked together like so many machines — in the interest of their powerful master, the Steel Trust.

Many of the armed guards were murderous criminals; penitentiary birds scraped together from the slums of the great cities to uphold Garyism by crushing real Americanism. They took advantage of the strike situation and the authority vested in them to indulge in an orgy of robbery and thievery. Dressed in United States army uniforms and wearing deputies' badges, they even robbed strikers in broad daylight on the main streets. And if the latter dared to protest they were lucky not to be beaten up, jailed and fined for disorderly conduct. The strike committees have records of many such cases. And worse yet, more than one striker was robbed while he was in jail. Liberty bonds and cash disappeared frequently. To lose watches, knives, etc., was a common occurrence.

Picketing was out of the question, although, like many other liberties denied the steel strikers, it is theoretically permitted under the laws and court rulings of Pennsylvania. Strikers foolhardy enough to attempt it were usually slugged and arrested. Even the right to strike was virtually overthrown. The practice was for several company and city police, without warrants, to seek a man in his home, crowd in and demand his return to work. Upon refusal he would be arrested and fined from $25 to $100 for disorderly conduct. Then he would be offered his money back, if he would agree to be a scab. This happened not once, but scores, if not hundreds of times. Like practices were engaged in almost everywhere. In Monessen State Police and other " peace officers " would regularly round up batches of strikers before the mill gates. Those that agreed to go to work were set free; the rest were jailed. Many were kept overnight in an old, unlighted building and threatened from time to time with hanging in the morning, if they would not become scabs. This was particularly terrifying, as the strikers, mainly foreigners knowing little of their supposed legal rights, had very good reason to think that State Police, as well as armed thugs, would go to any extreme against them. In Pittsburgh it-self, the decisive question asked petty prisoners in the police courts was, " Are you working? " Those who could show that they were strike-breakers were released forthwith; while those who admitted be-ing on strike were usually found guilty without further questioning. Throughout the whole dis-trict, to be a scab was to be a peaceable, law abid-ing citizen; to be a striker was criminal.

The courts put every obstacle in the way of the strikers getting justice. In those towns where it was possible to get lawyers at all no courtesies were extended the representatives of the men. They were denied the right of cross-examination; could not get the necessary papers for appeals, and in some cases were actually ordered out of court. Attorney Roe was arrested in McKeesport for attempting to confer with a dozen of his clients in a private hall. The strikers were held under excessive bail and fined shamefully for trivial charges, to disprove which they were often denied the right to produce wit-nesses. The following quotations from a report by J. G. Brown, formerly president of the International Union of Timber Workers, who was a general or-ganizer in the Pittsburgh district and later director of the legal department of the National Committee, will give an indication of the situation and some of the reasons therefor:

. . . The next day came the strike. The jails swarmed with arrested strikers. This was especially true in the Soho district of Pittsburgh, where are located the main entrances of the National Tube Works, and the Jones and Laughlin Company's plants. In the afternoon two

[136]

organizers who were walking down the street in this section were taken to jail, held without bail on charges of being "suspicious persons." Information was given to us that only the Supt. of Police had authority to fix bail. He could not be located. Indeed, that these men were arrested at all was learned only through the newspapers. They were not allowed to communicate with their friends or attorneys. Attorney Brennon eventually found the Chief of Police and went bail for the men.

Deciding to utilize the right of picketing, which the laws of the state permit, a group of men were chosen for this work, captains assigned and stationed at the entrances of the mills in Soho. No sooner had they arrived there than they were hustled right on to jail, which was already filled to overflowing. Many were convicted on disorderly conduct charges; others were warned of dire things in store for them, and all were advised to return to their work in the mills.

Many women and young girls were among the victims of police brutalities in the Soho district. Located in this section were only city policemen; the State Constabulary did not "work" much within the city limits. Much wonder was created by the undiminishing brutality of the Soho police. The Central Labor Council of Pittsburgh tried to have the City Council inaugurate an investigation of the shameful state of affairs, but nothing could be done.

Shortly after the strike was called off the Pittsburgh papers carried a story to the effect that the city policemen working in the Soho district had been "paid" $150 each by the National Tube Co. It was stated also that the same men were paid a like amount by the Jones and Laughlin Company. This explains, perhaps, why justice was so blind in this section.

On the opposite side of the Monongahela river, where

the Jones and Laughlin Company has other immense works the police were equally bad, the police magistrate even worse. The Police Commissioner was boss of the situation. And now come the Pittsburgh papers with the story that this very Commissioner, Peter P. Walsh, has made application to be retired from the Pittsburgh police force on half pay in order that he might accept the appointment as chief of the mill police of the Jones and Laughlin Company. The half pay allowance gives, according to reports, $1800 per year. The new position Mr. Walsh is to fill is popularly understood to carry with it a salary of $5000 per year. . . . The Central Labor Council is making an effort to have this matter investigated, but without serious hope of success.

When a labor committee demanded that Mayor Babcock of Pittsburgh investigate the situation, the honorable gentleman refused. He admitted that the action of the steel companies was ill-advised; the money should have been given to the pension fund, instead of to a few men; however, the matter was now past history, and there was nothing to be added to the fair name of Pittsburgh by airing it in public. The Mayor admitted, though, that he would object to having labor unions raise funds to pay policemen to favor them during strikes. So reason public officials in the steel districts.

Suppression of the rights of free speech and free assembly; gigantic organized campaigns of outlawry by the State Police and armies of selected plug-uglies; subornation and intimidation of city, county, state and federal officials and police; prostitution of the courts — these are some of the means used to crush the strike of the steel workers, and to force these over-worked, under-paid toilers still deeper into the mire of slavery. And the whole monstrous crime was hypocritically committed in the name of a militant, 100 per cent. Americanism.

IX

EFFORTS AT SETTLEMENT

THE NATIONAL INDUSTRIAL CONFERENCE — THE
SENATE COMMITTEE — THE RED BOOK — THE
MARGOLIS CASE — THE INTERCHURCH WORLD
MOVEMENT

UPON October 6 the National Industrial Conference
opened its sessions in Washington, D. C. This body
was called together by President Wilson to make an
effort to solve the pressing labor difficulties confronting the country, and was the one, pending whose
deliberations the steel workers had been asked to
postpone their strike. It was a three-party arrangement, Capital, Labor and the Public being represented. Naturally it was only advisory in character;
and under the rules adopted all action taken, not
relating merely to methods of procedure, had to have
the endorsement of all three sections, each of which
voted as a unit in accordance with the majority sentiment of its members.

The Conference met in the midst of a tense situation. The steel industry was almost completely
paralysed; the miners were just about to launch
their national general strike; the railroaders were
in a foment of discontent, and many other large and
important sections of workers were demanding

better conditions. Capital and Labor were arrayed against each other as never before. Both appeared determined to fight; Capital in a bitter, revengeful spirit to oust Labor from the favorable position won during the war, and Labor in a decided effort to hold what it had and to make more winnings to offset the rapidly mounting cost of living. The United States seemed upon the brink of an industrial war.

From the beginning the touchstone of the Conference, the measure by which all its activities were gauged, was the steel strike. It was clear that its attitude towards this great issue would settle its general policy. This was felt by all parties to the Conference, even though some hated the thought. The labor delegation, headed by Samuel Gompers, precipitated matters by introducing, by previous arrangement with the National Committee for Organizing Iron and Steel Workers, the following resolution:

WHEREAS, The Nation-wide strike now in progress in the steel industry of America affects not only the men and women directly concerned, but tends to disturb the relations between employers and workers throughout our industrial life; and

WHEREAS, This conference is called for the purpose of stabilizing industries and bringing into being a better relation between employers and employees; and

WHEREAS, Organized Labor wishes to manifest its sincere and fair desire to prove helpful in immediately adjusting this pending grave industrial conflict; therefore, be it,

RESOLVED, That each group comprising this conference select two of its number and these six so selected to constitute a committee to which shall be referred

[141]

existing differences between the workers and employers
in the steel industry for adjudication and settlement.
Pending the findings of this committee, this conference
requests the workers involved to return to work and
the employers to re-instate them in their former positions.

This resolution provoked a storm of opposition
from the reactionary employers, who, headed by Mr.
Gary (ironically seated with John D. Rockefeller,
Jr., as a representative of the Public) insisted that
the Conference ignore the steel strike situation altogether, its purpose being, according to them, not
the settlement of existing disputes, but the formula-
tion of principles and plans which would provide for
the prevention of such disputes in the future.   Finally, seeing that if they insisted upon their resolution
it would wreck the Conference, the workers held it
in abeyance temporarily and submitted the following:

> The right of wage earners to organize without dis-
> crimination, to bargain collectively, to be represented
> by representatives of their own choosing in negotiations
> and adjustments with employers in respect to wages,
> hours of labor and relations and conditions of employ-
> ment, is recognized.

Such a mild proposition as this would hardly meet
with serious opposition in a similar conference in any
other important country than ours. All over
Europe it would be far too conservative to fit the
situation. In England, for example, the British
Industrial Conference recently adopted the following:

[142]

The basis of negotiation between employers and work people should, as is presently the case in the chief industries of the country, be the full, frank acceptance of the employers' organizations on the one hand, and trade unions on the other as the recognized organizations to speak and act on behalf of their members.

And just across our border, in Canada, this advanced conception was formulated but a few months before:

On the whole we believe the day has passed when any employer should deny his employees the right to organize. Employers claim that right for themselves and it is not denied by the workers. There seems to be no reason why the employer should deny like rights to those who are employed by him. Not only should employees be accorded the right of organizing, but the prudent employer will recognize such organization and will deal with the duly accredited representatives thereof in all matters relating to the interests of the employees when it is fairly established to be representative of them all.

But Mr. Gary and his associates care nothing about the reputation of America as a progressive, liberty-loving country. They have their prerogatives, and they intend to exercise them, cost what it may. They organize as they see fit and pick out such representatives as they will; but by virtue of their economic strength they deny to their workers these same rights. So they voted down Labor's collective bargaining resolution, and at the same time the one providing for a settlement of the steel strike. The employers insisted upon absolute rule by themselves.

[143]

This action discredited the Conference, and sentenced it to dissolution. By its refusal to meet the great steel strike issue the Conference showed that it had neither the will nor the power to settle industrial disputes. Labor, openly denied the fundamental right of organization, could no longer sit with it. The workers' representatives, therefore, took the only honorable course left to them; they withdrew, allowing the whole worthless structure to collapse. Said Mr. Gompers in his final speech:

> Gentlemen, I have sung my swan song in this conference. You have, by your action — the action of the employers' group — legislated us out of this conference. We have nothing further to submit; and with a feeling of regret we have not been enabled with a clear conscience to remain here longer. We have responsibilities to employees and workers and those dependent upon them. We must fulfill these obligations.

Thus ingloriously ended the Conference upon which the steel workers had been asked to hang all their hopes. Even with powerful organizations intact and with their industry almost entirely at a standstill, the latter could get no consideration from it. What, then, would have been their fate if they had postponed the strike? With their forces shattered, half of their men being on strike and the rest at work thoroughly disgusted, they would have been helpless and unable to strike in any event. They would have been absolutely at the mercy of the employers. And any one who may imagine that the latter would have done anything short of giving the steel workers their *coup de grace* at the Confer-

[144]

ence is an optimist indeed. The steel strike was a clean fight and an honorable defeat for Labor. Its bad effects will soon wear off. But it would have been a ruinous calamity, with ineradicable harm, had the strike been postponed for the sake of the ill-fated Industrial Conference.

Pursuant to a resolution adopted by the Senate on September 23, in the white heat of the strike excitement, the Committee on Education and Labor was instructed to investigate the steel strike and to report back to the Senate as soon as possible. Accordingly this Committee held sittings in Washington and Pittsburgh, hearing about one hundred witnesses all told. Its active members were Senators Kenyon (Chairman), McKellar, Walsh (Mass.), Sterling and Phipps.

For the workers Samuel Gompers, John Fitzpatrick, M. F. Tighe and many organizers and strikers testified, setting forth in detail the grievances and demands of the men. For the steel companies came the usual crop of strike-breakers and company officials, pliable city authorities and business men from the steel towns. The star witness was Judge Gary, who presented practically the entire case for the whole steel industry. It is noteworthy that with the exception of one minor hothead, the so-called " independents " made no defense before the committee. They left it all to their master, the United States Steel Corporation.

Mr. Gary was a good witness. Not for him were the antiquated blusterings of a " divine-right " Baer or a " public-be-damned " Vanderbilt. He used the modern method,— a mass of silky hypocrisies and misrepresentations for the public, to cover up the mailed fist he has for his workers. He was suave, oily, humble, obliging, persuasive, patriotic. He pictured the steel industry as a sort of industrial heaven and the U. S. Steel Corporation as a beneficent institution, leading even the trade-union movement in reform work.

Inasmuch as Mr. Gary's peculiar notions of the " open shop," minority rule by the unions, etc., set forth afresh by him at the strike hearings, are discussed quite generally throughout this book, there is no need to review them again here. We will note his testimony no more than to give the facts of the death of Mrs. Fannie Sellins, of whose murder he was so anxious to clear the Steel Trust.

Mrs. Fannie Sellins was an organizer for the United Mine Workers of America, stationed in the notorious, anti-union Black Valley district along the Allegheny river. An able speaker, and possessed of boundless courage, energy, enthusiasm and idealism, she was a most effective worker. Due largely to her efforts many thousands of miners and miscellaneous workers in this hard district were organized. She was the very heart of the local labor movement, which ranked second to none in Pennsylvania for spirit and progress. When the steel campaign began, Mrs. Sellins threw herself wholeheartedly into it. She worked indefatigably. More than any other individual she was responsible for the unionization of the big United States Steel Corporation mills at Vandergrift, Leechburgh and New Kensington, as well as those of the so-called inde-

[146]

pendent Allegheny and West Penn Steel Companies at Brackenridge. The results secured by her will compare favorably with those of any other organizer in the whole campaign.

By her splendid work in behalf of the toilers Mrs. Sellins gained the undying hatred of the untamed employers in the benighted Black Valley district. Open threats were made to " get " her. The opportunity came on August 26, 1919, when she was deliberately murdered under the most brutal circumstances.

The miners of the Allegheny Coal and Coke Company were on strike at West Natrona. The mine is situated in the mill yard of the Allegheny Steel Company and furnishes fuel for that concern. All was going peacefully when a dozen drunken deputy sheriffs on strike duty, led by a mine official, suddenly rushed the pickets, shooting as they came. Joseph Strzelecki fell, mortally wounded. Mrs. Sellins, standing close by, rushed first to get some children out of danger. Then she came back to plead with the deputies, who were still clubbing the prostrate Strzelecki, not to kill him. What happened then is told in the *New Majority* (Chicago) of September 20:

—— ——, the mine official, snatched a club and felled the woman to the ground.

This was not on company ground, but just outside the fence of a friend of Mrs. Sellins.

She rose and tried to drag herself toward the gate. —— shouted: " Kill that — — — — — —! "

Three shots were fired, each taking effect.

She fell to the ground, and —— cried: " Give her another! "

[147]

One of the deputies, standing over the motionless and silent body, held his gun down and, without averting his face, fired into the body that did not move.

An auto truck, in waiting, was hurried to the scene and the body of the old miner thrown in; then Mrs. Sellins was dragged by the heels to the back of the car. Before she was placed in the truck, a deputy took a cudgel and crushed in her skull before the eyes of the throng of men, women and children, who stood in powerless silence before the armed men. Deputy ——— picked up the woman's hat, placed it on his head, danced a step, and said to the crowd: " I'm Mrs. Sellins now."

Thus perished noble Fannie Sellins: shot in the back by so-called peace officers. And she 49 years old, a grandmother, and mother of a boy killed in France, fighting to make the world safe for democracy.

Many people witnessed this ·horrible murder. The guilty men were named openly in the newspapers and from a hundred platforms. Yet no one was ever punished for the crime. Witnesses were spirited away or intimidated, and the whole matter hushed up in true Steel Trust fashion. A couple of deputies were arrested; but they were speedily released on smaller bonds than those often set for strikers arrested for picketing. Eventually they were freed altogether.

The killing of Mrs. Sellins, right in the teeth of the strike as it was, lent much bitterness to the general situation. Rightly or wrongly, the steel workers, almost to a man, felt that this devoted woman was a martyr to their cause.

[148]

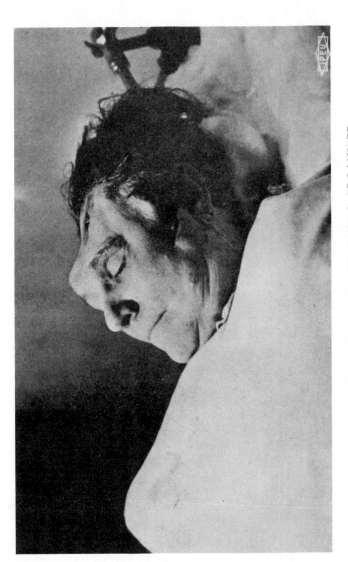

MRS. FANNIE SELLINS, TRADE UNION ORGANIZER
Killed by Steel Trust gunmen, West Natrona, Pa., Aug. 26, 1919.

Upon November 8, the Senate Committee, having completed its hearings, made public its report. This document is a strange mixture of progressive and reactionary principles. In some respects, especially where it grants, however confusedly, the right of collective bargaining and the eight hour day, it is just and meets the situation; but in other respects it is so unfair to the workers' cause as to be grotesque. For one thing it shoulders upon the unions the entire responsibility for the failure to postpone the strike, choosing to disregard completely the clearly established fact that the steel companies were discharging men so fast that for the unions it was a case of strike or perish. In fact, the report ignores altogether the bitter grievance of men being discharged for union membership. Mr. Gary had said that this practice was not engaged in, and that apparently settled it so far as the Committee was concerned,— the testimony of dozens of victimized workers (with thousands more available) to the contrary notwithstanding. Other sins of the Steel Trust, the suppression of free speech and free assembly, etc., were passed over lightly; but the alleged virtues of its housing and welfare plans were very highly lauded.

Nowhere are the workers more ruthlessly robbed and exploited by their employers than in the steel industry. Speaking recently in Brooklyn on the subject of profiteering, Mr. Basil Manly, formerly Joint Chairman of the National War Labor Board, cited Page 367 of the Treasury report as showing one steel company " earning " $14,549,952 in 1917 on a capital of $5,000, or a profit of 290,999 per cent. As the department conveniently suppresses all details, it is impossible to learn the name of this company or how it made such fabulous profits. On the same page appeared another steel company with a profit rate of 20,180 per cent. Speaking of the United States Steel Corporation's returns, which of course were garbled so that no outsider could understand them, Mr. Manly said:

> For this reason I am unable to tell you, on the basis of the Treasury Department's figures, what the net income of the Steel Corporation is, but on the basis of its own published report I can tell you that in two years, 1916 and 1917, the net profits of the Steel Corporation, after payment of interest on bonds and after making allowance for all charges growing out of the installation of special war facilities, amounted to $888,931,511. This is more by $20,000,000 than the total capital stock of the Steel Corporation (which is $868,583,600). In other words, in 1916 and 1917 every dollar of the capital stock of the Steel Corporation was paid for in net profits. In this connection it should be remembered that when the Steel Corporation was formed its entire $500,000,000 worth of common stock represented nothing but water.

The other steel companies did as well or better, proportionately. W. Jett Lauck, acting on behalf of the railroad workers, submitted figures to the United States Railroad Labor Board (A. P. dispatches May 19, 1920) showing that during the years 1916–18 the Bethlehem Steel Corporation " earned " average annual profits of $29,000,000, or six times its pre-war average. In 1916 its profits amounted to 146 per cent. on its capital stock. Our

Johnstown friend, the Cambria Steel Company, in 1916–17 cleaned up $50,000,000 on $45,000,000 capital stock; while the Lackawanna, Republic, Colorado Fuel and Iron, Jones and Laughlin, Crucible, etc., companies made similar killings.

As against useless, non-producing drones getting these millions, the great mass of workers actually operating the industry were receiving the beggarly wages of from 42 to 48 cents per hour. They had received no increase for a year before the strike, notwithstanding the skyrocketing cost of living. Yet the Senate Committee could discover no discontent at this condition nor see any injustice in it. Upon page 10 of its report appears the startling statement that " The question of wages is not involved in this controversy." Forty-two cents per hour would hardly buy cigars for these smug, well-fed gentlemen; still they would have us conclude that it is enough for a steel worker to raise a family upon.

The fact is, of course, that an increase in wages was a cardinal demand of the strikers, even though the Senate Committee did not get to learn of it.[1] And so great was the steel workers' need for more

[1] There seemed to be many important things of which this committee had never heard. For instance, when in my testimony I referred to Lester F. Ward, Senator Sterling innocently inquired who he was. He had apparently never even heard of this eminent American sociologist, who was perhaps the greatest scholar ever born in the western hemisphere, and whose name is honored by scientific minds the world over. And what makes Senator Sterling's ignorance the more inexcusable is that he was actually holding office in Washington at the same time that Professor Ward was carrying on his brilliant studies in that very city. For one who stresses so much his 100 per cent. Americanism as does the Senator it is indeed a sad showing not to be familiar with this great native product.

[151]

money that the strike had scarcely ended when the United States Steel Corporation, followed soon after by the "independents," granted .its lesser skilled help 10 per cent. increase in wages, and promised "an equitable adjustment" to the widely advertised small minority of highly paid men.

Part of the strike-breaking strategy of the Steel Trust was to alienate public sympathy from the strike by denouncing it as an incipient revolution which had to be put down at all costs. Public opinion was already violently inflamed against everything savoring no matter how slightly of radicalism, and it was not difficult for the re-actionary newspapers to make the steel strike unpopular, even as they had, under various pretexts, the movements of the miners and railroad men of the period. One weapon they used extensively against the steel strike was an almost forgotten pamphlet, "Syndicalism," written by Earl C. Ford and myself eight years ago.

Throughout the hearings the investigating senators went along with this Steel Trust propaganda, which was not so surprising considering the fact that of the five active committee men, one was a steel magnate, and three others typical Bourbons. By playing up the "little red book" they systematically fed the newspapers with the sensationalism they wanted and which the steel companies desired them to get. I was called before the Committee and gruffly ordered to express my opinion on the doctrines in the booklet. In reply, I stated that the steel movement had been carried on according to the strictest trade-union principles. It was overseen by the National Committee, consisting of twenty-four presidents of large international unions. As secretary of this committee I had necessarily worked under the close scrutiny of these men and dozens of their organizers — not to speak of the highest officials in the American Federation of Labor. Yet none of these trade unionists, keen though they be to detect and condemn unusual practices and heresy in the ranks, had found fault with the character of my work. Nor could the crew of detectives and stool pigeons of the steel companies and Department of Justice, who had dogged my footsteps for a year past, cite a single word said, a thing done, or a line written by me in the entire campaign which would not measure up to most rigid trade-union standards. I contended that my private opinions were immaterial as they did not and could not enter into the organizing work or the strike.

But the nation-wide head hunt of the radicals was on in full cry, and the Senators had a good blood scent. They would follow it to the end. They insisted that I express my opinion upon the wage system, the state, morality, patriotism, marriage, etc. Finally, in a last effort to protect the interests of the 2,000,000 men, women and childen affected by the strike, I stated that if the vulture press, which was bound to misrepresent what I said, was removed from the room, I would be glad to oblige the Senators with a frank expression of my views upon any subject. But this simple fairness to the steel workers and their families they denied. The newspapers were clamoring for red meat, and the Senators seemed determined they should have it. Having made my protest and my prediction, I was compelled to yield; but the first newspapers on the streets proved the soundness of my fears. My answers were garbled and twisted against both the steel movement and me.

Then there was the Margolis case. I charge that to be a deliberate frameup against the steel strike. To prove the Steel Trust's contention that the strike was a desperate revolutionary *coup*, engineered by men seeking to destroy our civilization generally, somewhat more was required than merely an eight year old booklet. The thing had to be brought down to date and a far-reaching plot constructed. Hence the Senate Committee dragged in Mr. Margolis and made him a scapegoat. Mr. Margolis is a well known Anarchist attorney of Pittsburgh. He has the reputation of having served ably as counsel for several trade-union organizations, and has a wide circle of acquaintances among labor men. The Senate Committee selected him as the man who had organized, with my hearty support and co-operation, the real force behind the strike, the I. W. W.'s, Anarchists and Bolshevists.

Now the fact is that Mr. Margolis had nothing whatever to do, officially or unofficially, with the policies or management of either the organizing campaign or the strike. He had no connection with the Strike committee; nor did he ever even speak at a union meeting of steel workers during the whole movement in question. If he wrote an article in some radical paper, or spoke to a meeting of Russian workmen in Youngstown, endorsing the strike, as is said, he did it purely as an individual sympathizer acting upon his own initiative. Mr. Margolis freely

[154]

stated this on the stand, and every union official in Pittsburgh knew it to be the case. So did the investigating Senators; but it the better served their purpose to enlarge upon Mr. Margolis' activities, in the hope that his radical reputation would lend color to the plot theory which they were laboring so hard to establish, and which was so advantageous to the Steel Trust.

In their final report the Senators continued their plot " evidence " and insinuations, so persistently worked up all through their hearings. They ignored highly important testimony tending to put the movement in its right light as a strictly trade-union affair, and gave prominence to everything to the contrary. They elevated unheard-of I. W. W.'s into powerful strike leaders and surrounded the most ordinary comings and goings with revolutionary mystery. Where they lacked facts they cast suspicion, leaving a vicious daily press to draw its own conclusions.

Although they expressed great concern for the sufferings of the public in strikes, and advocated the establishment of an industrial tribunal to prevent them in the future, the worthy Senators, nevertheless, recommended no means to end the steel strike. So far as they were concerned, apparently they were willing to have the steel strike fought to a conclusion. At one of the Senate Committee hearings, John Fitzpatrick, Chairman of the National Committee, agreed to arbitration. But later Mr. Gary gave an emphatic " No " to this proposition. Mr. Gary's wishes usually had decisive weight with the Senators, so the matter was settled.

[155]

On October 1–3, 1919, a national conference called by the Industrial Relations Department of the Interchurch World Movement met at the Hotel Pennsylvania in New York and adopted a resolution providing for a full investigation of the steel strike, then a burning public question. Under the terms of this resolution the Industrial Relations Department set up an independent Commission of Inquiry, composed of representative churchmen from all over the country who should be responsible for carrying out the investigation. This Commission consisted of Bishop Francis J. McConnell (Methodist), Chairman, Dr. Daniel A. Poling (Evangelical), vice-Chairman, Dr. John McDowell (Presbyterian), Mrs. Fred Bennett (Board of Foreign Missions), Dr. Nicholas Van Der Pyl (Congregational), Dr. Alva W. Taylor (Disciples), and Mr. Geo. W. Coleman (Baptist).

In order to commit the investigation of technical data to the hands of trained men, the Industrial Relations Department obtained the services of the Bureau of Industrial Research, New York, which, besides its own researches, obtained the co-operation of various other scientific agencies and organized a staff of field workers whose principal members were: Mr. George Soule, Mr. David J. Saposs, Miss Marian D. Savage, Mr. Marion K. Wisehart and Mr. Robert Littell. A member of the Bureau of Industrial Research, Mr. Heber Blankenhorn, had charge of the field work and later acted as Secretary to the Commission of Inquiry, which held hearings in Pittsburgh, Chicago, and other steel centres.

The Interchurch World Movement, representing

as it does the organized Protestant millions of America, is a conservative and respectable body, if there is such in this country. Yet when it stepped upon the toes of the Steel Trust by starting the investigation it found itself soon classed among the revolutionaries. Persistent rumors were sent broadcast, and even newspaper stories, to the effect that the Commission's investigators were " Bolsheviks " and that the Interchurch World Movement was permeated with " anarchists." This hampered the work greatly, especially among employers. Finally a threat of legal action was necessary against a large commercial organization which had circulated the rumors officially. It eventually retracted in full. As for the workers, they gave the fullest co-operation to the investigation.

Impressed by the scientific methods and apparent desire to get at the truth of the strike situation manifested in the Interchurch investigation — which stood in striking contrast to the slipshod, haphazard system, " red " mania, and violent partiality towards the steel companies shown by the Senate Committee, — the strike leaders decided to ask the Commission to undertake a settlement of the strike by mediation, which the Commission had the power to do under the resolution creating it. The workers' representatives felt that no stone should be left unturned to get a settlement, and that if the powerful Interchurch movement stirred in their behalf possibly Mr. Gary would be dislodged from his position.

Consequently, John Fitzpatrick, Chairman of the National Committee, put before Mr. Blankenhorn a plan for the settlement of the strike by mediation.

Mr. Blankenhorn felt, however, that it might be better to recommend that the Commission move independently, rather than as merely representing the strikers, and submitted the following plan, which was adopted by the Commission:

1. To mediate in behalf of all the steel workers, both those on strike and those who had gone back to work.
2. That the purpose of the mediation should be to establish a new deal in the steel industry rather than merely to end the strike.
3. That the ending of the strike should be arranged solely with a view to giving the new deal the best possible chance.

On December 1, the National Committee for Organizing Iron and Steel Workers met and formally accepted this proposition of mediation. What happened next is told in an official statement to the writer of this book:

On December 5 a committee from the Commission, consisting of Bishop McConnell, Dr. Poling and Dr. McDowell, called on Mr. Gary with the purpose of, first, ascertaining if he would accept their office as mediators; next, of proposing their plan of mediation and pressing the acceptance of it by the employers; and, finally, of ordering the men back to work, the strike leaders to step out of the situation, and the Commission to set up a permanent mediation body to bring about a conference between employers and employees in the steel industry. There was the feeling in the Commission that extraordinary concessions had been made by the leaders of the strike and that any reasons advocated by the employers for not accepting the mediation plan would have to be weighty.

Mr. Gary received the Commission courteously and after minutely cross-examining them concerning the " anonymous " report of the presence of " Bolsheviks " among them, he heard the Commission to the extent of learning the first step in their proposal. He made his reply immediately, an absolute refusal of arbitration or mediation. The Commission therefore never had any opportunity to present the authorized acceptance of the mediation plan by the other side and in no sense conveyed to Mr. Gary the extent of the concessions which the strikers were then willing to make. Mr. Gary, however, clearly understood that acceptance of the mediation plan would mean that the men would all return to work at once.

Mr. Gary based his refusal on the grounds that any dealings which in any way involved representatives of the men then on strike would be an acceptance of the closed shop, sovietism, and the forcible distribution of property. Mr. Gary said that if the Commission represented the men who had gone back to work, those men were content; if the Commission represented the men who had not gone back to work, those men are nothing but red radicals whom the plants did not want anyway. He said that there was absolutely no issue for discussion with the U. S. Steel Corporation.

The Commission presented its view-point on the advisability of mediation at great length and with insistence. Mr. Gary did not in any respect modify his immediate decision.

The Commission felt it necessary therefore to drop the plan and transmitted the following to the National Committee:

December 6, 1919

Memorandum for Mr. Fitzpatrick:

The independent Commission of Inquiry, instituted by the Interchurch World Movement to investigate the steel strike, received on December 2 a communication marked "confidential," dealing with an official action taken by the National Committee for Organizing Iron and Steel Workers, signed by Mr. Fitzpatrick and Mr. Foster.

On December 5, members of the Commission informally conversed with Mr. Gary for two hours, proposing to plan a new basis of relations in the steel industry, with an ending of the strike best calculated to further better relations. They offered to act as mediators both on behalf of the men still on strike, whose leaders were to order them back and then step out of the situation, and on behalf of still dissatisfied men who had nevertheless returned to work.

Mr. Gary refused to confer with these representatives of the churches as mediators in behalf of any interests represented by you in the strike, on the ground that the men still out were Bolshevist radicals who were not wanted in the mills and who would not be taken back.

And as to mediating in behalf of any other interests, Mr. Gary said that the men were contented and that "there is no issue."

I am requested to communicate the above information to you by the Chairman of the Commission of Inquiry.

Very truly yours,
H. BLANKENHORN.

At the time this book goes to press the findings and recommendations of the Commission have not yet been made public.

This made the sixth attempt of the National Committee to settle the steel controversy — not to mention the individual effort of the Amalgamated Association. They were: (1) The letter from Mr.

Gompers to Mr. Gary requesting a conference; (2) the visit to his office of the National Committee conference committee, equipped with the power to set a strike date; (3) the appeal to President Wilson to arrange a conference; (4) Organized Labor's resolution in the National Industrial Conference to have that body select an arbitration board; (5) The offer of arbitration by John Fitzpatrick while testifying before the Senate Committee; and, (6) the Interchurch mediation incident.

But they were all futile. Mr. Gary's policy is the time-honored one of all tyrants, rule or ruin. The unions had no option but to fight, and this they did to the best of their ability.

X

THE COURSE OF THE STRIKE

PITTSBURGH DISTRICT — THE RAILROAD MEN — CORRUPT NEWSPAPERS — CHICAGO DISTRICT — FEDERAL TROOPS AT GARY — YOUNGSTOWN DISTRICT — THE AMALGAMATED ASSOCIATION — CLEVELAND — THE ROD AND WIRE MILL STRIKE — THE BETHLEHEM PLANTS — BUFFALO AND LACKAWANNA — WHEELING AND STEUBENVILLE — PUEBLO — JOHNSTOWN — MOB RULE — THE END OF THE STRIKE.

ALTHOUGH the Steel strike was national in scope and manifested the same general, basic tendencies everywhere, nevertheless it differed enough from place to place to render necessary some indication of particular events in the various districts in order to convey a clear conception of the movement as a whole. It is the purpose of this chapter to point out a few of these salient features in the several localities and to draw some lessons therefrom.

In the immediate Pittsburgh district, due to the extreme difficulties under which the organizing work was carried on and the strike inaugurated, the shutdown was not so thorough as elsewhere. Considerable numbers of men, notably in the skilled trades, remained at work, and the mills limped along, at least pretending to operate. This was exceedingly bad, Pittsburgh being the strategic centre of the strike, as it is of the industry, and the companies were making tremendous capital of the fact that the mills there were still producing steel. Accordingly, the National Committee left no stone unturned to complete the tie-up, already 75 per cent. effective. But under the circumstances, with meetings banned and picketing prohibited, it was out of the question to reach directly the men who had stayed at work. The key to the situation was in the hands of the railroad men.

Operating between the various steel plants and connecting them up with the main lines, there are several switching roads, such as the Union Railroad and the McKeesport and Monongahela Connecting Lines. They are the nerve centers of the local steel industry. If they could be struck the mills would have to come to a stand-still. The National Committee immediately delegated organizers to investigate the situation. These reported that the body of the men in the operating departments were organized; that they had no contracts with the steel companies, and that they were ready for action, but awaiting co-operation from their respective national headquarters.

Consequently, the National Committee arranged a conference in Washington with responsible representatives of the Brotherhoods and laid the situation before them. In reply they stated that their policy was strictly to observe their contracts wherever they had such, and that their men would be forbidden to do work around the mills not done by them prior to the strike. It was up to the men on the non-contract roads and yards to decide for themselves about joining the strike. We informed them then that the situation was such, with the men scattered through many locals, that merely leaving it up to them was insufficient; it would be impossible for them to act together without direct aid and encouragement from their higher officials. We made the specific request that each of the organizations send a man into Pittsburgh to take a strike vote of the men in question, who are all employees of the steel companies. They took the matter under advisement; but nothing came of it, although long afterwards, when the opportune moment had passed, organizer J. M. Patterson of the Railway Carmen (also of the Trainmen) was authorized to take a strike vote. Thus was lost the chance to close down these strategic switching lines and with them, in all likelihood, several big mills in the most vital district in the entire steel industry.

Throughout the strike zone general disappointment was expressed by the steel workers at the apparent lack of sympathy with their cause shown by the officials of the Brotherhoods. The steel workers, bitterly oppressed for a generation and fighting desperately towards the light in the face of unheard-of opposition, turned instinctively for aid to their closely related, powerfully organized fellow workers, the railroad men. And the latter could easily have lent them effective, if not decisive assistance without violating a contract or in any way endangering their standing. It was not to be expected that the trunk line men, working as they were under government agreements, would refuse to haul the scab steel; but there were many other ways, perfectly legitimate under current trade-union practice and ethics, in which help could have been given; yet it was not. From Youngstown and elsewhere the railroad men who did go on strike in the mill yards complained with bitterness that they were neglected and denied strike benefits, and that the rule that no road man should do work around the mills not customary before the strike was flagrantly violated. Usually the rank and file were strongly disposed to assist the hard-pressed steel workers, and they could have everywhere wonderfully stiffened the strike, but the necessary encouragement and cooperation from the several headquarters was lacking. Truth demands that these unpleasant things be set down. Labor can learn and progress only through a frank acknowledgment and discussion of its weaknesses, mistakes and failures.

In addition to all their other handicaps the Pittsburgh district strikers had to contend with a particularly treacherous local press. Everywhere our daily papers are newspapers only by courtesy of a misapplied term. They are sailing under false colors. Pretending to be purveyors of unbiased accounts of current happenings, they are in reality merely propaganda organs, twisting, garbling and suppressing facts and information in the manner best calculated to further the interests of the employing class. The whole newsgathering and distributing system is a gigantic mental prostitution. Consequently, considering the issues involved, it was not surprising to see the big daily papers take such a decided stand against the steel workers. Everywhere in steel districts the papers were bad enough, but those in the Pittsburgh district outstripped all the rest. They gave themselves over body and soul to the service of the Steel Trust.

From the first these Pittsburgh papers were violently antagonistic to the steel workers. Every sophistry uttered by Mr. Gary to the effect that the strike was an effort to establish the " closed shop," a bid for power, or an attempt at revolution, the papers echoed and re-echoed *ad nauseum*. They played up the race issue, virtually advising the Americans to stand together against the foreigners who were about to overwhelm them. They painted the interests of the country as being synonymous with those of the steel companies and tried to make Americanism identical with scabbery. For them no further proof of one's patriotism was needed than to go back to the mills. Every clubbing of strikers was the heroic work of the law-abiding against reckless mobs. Strike " riots " were manufactured out of whole cloth. For instance, when the senators investigating the strike were visiting the Homestead mills, a couple of strike-breakers quarreling with each other, several blocks away, fired a shot. An hour later screaming headlines told the startled populace of Pittsburgh that " STRIKERS SHOOT AT SENATORS " and " MOB ATTACKS SENATE COMMITTEE." Even the stand-pat senators had to protest that this was going it too strong.

In revenge for an alleged dynamiting in Donora, Pa., the authorities swooped down upon the union headquarters, arrested 101 strikers present, including organizer Walter Hodges, and charged them with the crime. Since there was not a shred of evidence against the accused, they were all eventually discharged. Then the Donora *Herald,* which forever yelped that the organizers advocated violence, had this to say:

> One of the reasons we have sedition preached in America is because we have grand juries like that at Washington (Pa.) this week which ignored the dynamiting cases. Possibly the biggest mistake of all was made in not using rifles at the time instead of turning the guilty parties over to the very sensitive mercies of the grand jury.

But the journalistic strike-breaking master-stroke was an organized effort to stampede the men back to work by minimizing the strike's effectiveness. First the papers declared that only a few thousands of Pittsburgh's steel workers went out. Then they followed this for weeks with stories of thousands of men flocking back to the mills. Full page advertisements begged the men to go back; while flaming headlines told us that " MEN GO BACK TO MILLS," " STEEL STRIKE WANING," " MILLS OPERATING STRONGER," " MORE MEN GO BACK TO WORK," etc. It became a joke, but the patient Pittsburgh people couldn't see it. Said Wm. Hard in the *Metropolitan* for February, 1920:

> " Mr. Foster," I said, " I am going to be perfectly frank with you. I know your strike's a fizzle of course, but I know more. I not only take pains to

[167]

read the telegraphic dispatches of the news from the managers of the steel mills, but I keep the clippings. I have the history of your strike in cold print. Hardly anybody struck anyhow, in most places, except some foreigners; and then they began at once to go back in thousands and thousands and new thousands every day for months. If you claim there were 300,000 strikers, I don't care. I've counted up the fellows that went back to work, and I've totalled them up day by day. They're a little over 4,800,000. So you're pretty far behind."

But despite everything — the suppression of free speech and free assembly, Cossack terrorism, official tyranny, prostitution of the courts, attacks from the lying press, and all the rest of it — the steel workers in the immediate Pittsburgh district (comprising the towns along the Allegheny and Monongahela rivers from Apollo to Monessen) made a splendid fight. The very pressure seemed to hold them the better together. Their ranks were never really broken, the strike being weakened only by a long, costly wearing-away process. The stampede back to work, so eagerly striven for by the employers, did not materialize. In the beginning of the strike the Pittsburgh district was the weakest point in the battle line; at the end it was one of the very strongest.

The Chicago district struck very well, but it weakened earlier than others. This was because the employers scored a break-through at Indiana Harbor and Gary, particularly the latter place, which shattered the whole line.

Gary, the great western stronghold of the United

States Steel Corporation, was the storm center of the Chicago district at all times. Hardly had the organization campaign begun in 1918, when the Gary *Tribune* bitterly assailed the unions, accusing them of advocating evasion of the draft, discouragement of liberty bond sales, and general opposition to the war program. These lies were run in a full page editorial in English, and repeated in a special eight page supplement containing sixteen languages, a half page to each. Many thousands of copies were scattered broadcast. Other attacks in a similar vein followed. It was a foul blast straight from the maw of the Steel Trust. Incidentally it created a situation which shows how the steel men control public opinion.

The new unions immediately boycotted the *Tribune*. Result: the Gary *Post,* somewhat friendly inclined, doubled its circulation at once. The *Post* then became more friendly; whereupon, it is alleged, a leading banker called the editor to his office and told him that if he did not take a stand against the unions his credit would be stopped, which would have meant suspension within the week. That very day the *Post* joined the *Tribune's* campaign of abuse. Apparently the *Post's* youthful editor had learned a new wrinkle in journalism.

The Steel Trust did all it could to hold Gary from unionizing; but when the strike came the walkout was estimated to be 97 per cent. At first everything went peacefully, but the Steel Corporation was watching for an opportunity to get its strategic Gary mills into operation. The occasion presented itself on October 4, when strikers coming from a meeting

[169]

fell foul of some homeward bound scabs. Local labor men declare the resultant scrimmage " did not make as much disturbance as ordinarily would occur in a saloon when two or three men were fighting." It was a trivial incident — a matter for the police. Only one man was injured, and he very slightly. But the inspired press yelled red murder and pictured the hospitals as full of wounded. The militia were ordered in. The unions offered to furnish 700 ex-service men to enforce law and order; but this was rejected. Later the militia were transferred to Indiana Harbor; on October 6, a provisional regiment of regular troops, under command of General Leonard Wood, came to Gary from nearby Fort Sheridan, and martial law was at once proclaimed. The Steel Corporation now had the situation in hand; and the Gary strike was doomed.

Grave charges were voiced against the misuse made of the Federal troops in Gary. John Fitzpatrick writes me as follows, basing his statements upon reliable witnesses:

Now we have military control, the city of Gary being placed under martial law. The strike leaders and pickets were arrested by the soldiers and put to work splitting wood and sweeping the streets. This was most humiliating, because the camp was across the street from the city hall and in the most frequented part of the city.

When street-sweeping here did not break their spirits, these men were taken to the back streets, where they had their homes and where their own and the neighbor's children watched them through the windows.

The so-called foreigners have great respect for law

[170]

and authority, especially military authority, which plays such a big part in their native environments. The U. S. Steel Corporation did not fail to take advantage of this. In the first place they gave out the impression that the letters " U. S." in the corporation's name indicated that it was owned by the U. S. Government, and that the Government soldiers being in town meant that any one interfering with the steel company's affairs would be deported or sent to Fort Leavenworth.

Then a mill superintendent would take a squad of soldiers and go to the home of a striker. The soldiers would be lined up in front of the house; the superintendent would go in. He would tell John that he came to give him his last chance to return to work, saying that if he refused he would either go to jail or be deported. Then he would take John to the window and show him the row of soldiers. John would look at the wife and kids and make up his mind that his first duty was to them; that was what the strike was for anyway. So he would put on his coat and go back to the mills. Then the superintendent would go to the next house and repeat the performance.

Such tactics, coupled with spectacular midnight raids to " unearth " the widely advertised " red " plotters,— conveniently ignored until the strike,— the suppression of meetings, limitations on picketing, and the hundred forms of studied intimidation practiced by the soldiery, in a few weeks broke the backbone of the strike. And while the regular troops operated so successfully and systematically against the workers in Gary, the militia did almost as well in Indiana Harbor, where the strike also cracked.

The great re-actionary interests which backed General Wood for the Republican presidential nomination, including the Steel Trust, are giving him boundless credit for breaking the steel strike in Gary. Consequently there are many workers who believe the whole affair was staged to further his political fortunes. If not, how did it happen that the militia, who could have handled the situation easily, were sent out of Gary to make room for his regulars? And why was it that before there was a sign of trouble General Wood had formed his provisional regiment, shipped it from Fort Dodge to Fort Sheridan, and made other active preparations to invade Gary? And then, how did it come that he took charge of the situation in person, when at best it was only a colonel's job? In fact, how about the whole wretched business? Was it merely a political stunt to give General Wood the publicity that came to him for it?

The collapse at Gary and Indiana Harbor affected adversely South Chicago and almost the whole Chicago district. Worse still, it weakened the morale everywhere; and thus undermined, the strike rapidly disintegrated. By the middle of November, district secretary De Young reported that all the mills in the district, except those in Joliet and Waukegan, were working crews from 50 to 85 per cent. of normal, although, due to green hands and demoralized working forces, production averaged considerably lower. And the situation gradually grew worse. Joliet and Waukegan, however, held fast to the end, making a fight comparable with that of the men in Peoria and Hammond, who had gone out several weeks before September 22. It was at the latter place that police and company guards brutally shot down and killed four strikers on September 9.

In the immediate Youngstown district the strike was highly effective, hardly a ton of steel being produced anywhere for several weeks. This was due largely to the walkout of the railroad men employed in the mill yards, who acted on their own volition. Many of these belonged to the Brotherhoods, and others to the Switchmen's Union, while some were unorganized; but all struck together. Then they held joint mass meetings, got an agreement from the A. F. of L. unions that they would be protected and represented in any settlement made, and stuck loyally to the finish. They were a strong mainstay of the strike.

The weakening of the strike began about November 15. In a number of plants, notably those of the Trumbull Steel Company and the Sharon Steel Hoop Company, the Amalgamated Association of Iron, Steel and Tin Workers had agreements covering the skilled steel making trades, but when the laborers struck these skilled men had to quit also. The break in the district came when the Amalgamated Association virtually forced the laborers back to work in these shops in order to get them in operation. This action its officials justified by the following clause in their agreements:

> It was agreed that when a scale or scales are signed in general or local conferences, said scales or contracts shall be considered inviolate for that scale year, and should the employees of any departments (who do not

[173]

come under the above named scales or contracts) become members of the Amalgamated Association during
the said scale year, the Amalgamated Association may
present a scale of wages covering said employees, but
in case men and management cannot come to an agreement on said scale, same shall be held over until the
next general or local conference, and all men shall
continue work until the expiration of the scale year.

Relying upon their rights under this clause, the
companies naturally refused to give the laborers any
consideration whatever until the end of the scale
year. This meant that the latter were told to work
and wait until the following June, when their grievances would be taken up. The result was disastrous; the laborers generally lost faith in the Amalgamated Association, feeling that they had been
sacrificed for the skilled workers. They began to
flock back to work in all the plants. Then men in
other trades took the position that it was foolish
for them to fight on, seeing that the Amalgamated
Association was forcing its men back into the mills.
A general movement millward set in. By December
10 the strike was in bad shape. In passing it may
be noted that in Pittsburgh and other places where
it had contracts, the Amalgamated Association took
the same action, with the same general results, although not so extensive and harmful as in the
Youngstown district. In Cleveland the charters
were taken from local unions that refused to abide
by this clause.

The other trades affiliated with the National
Committee protested against the enforcement of the
clause. They declared it to be invalid, because it

violated trade-union principles and fundamental human rights. Seeing that no consideration was given the laborers under the agreement, their right to strike should have been preserved inviolate. It verged upon peonage to tie them up with an agreement that gave them no protection yet deprived them of the right to defend themselves. These trades freely predicted that to enforce the clause would break the strike in the Youngstown district, as it was altogether out of the question to ask men who had been on strike two months (especially men inexperienced in unionism) to resume work upon such conditions. But all arguments were vain; the Amalgamated Association officials were as adamant. They held their agreements with the employers to be sacred and to rank above any covenants they had entered into with the co-operating trades. They would enforce them to the letter — the interests of the laborers, the mechanical trades, and even the strike itself, to the contrary notwithstanding. Being a federated body, the National Committee had to bow to this decision and stand by, helpless, while its effects worked havoc with the strike.

Into Youngstown, in common with all the other districts, armies of scabs were poured. It was the policy of the United States Steel Corporation to operate, or at least to pretend to operate its mills, regardless of cost. So all the " independents " had to do likewise. Word came to the National Committee of several companies which, rather than try to run with the high-priced, worthless strikebreakers, would have been glad either to settle with the unions or to close their plants. But they were afraid to do

[175]

either; Gary had said " Operate," and it was a case of do that or risk going out of business.

The demand for scabs was tremendous. Probably half the strike-breaking agencies in the country were engaged in recruiting them. Thousands of negroes were brought from the South, and thousands of guttersnipe whites from the big northern cities. But worst of all were the skilled steel workers from outlying sections. There were many of such men who went on strike in their own home towns, sneaked away to other steel centres and worked there until the strike was over. Then they would return to their old jobs with cock-and-bull stories (for the workers only) of having worked in other industries, thus seeking to escape the dreaded odium of being known as scabs. These contemptible cowards, being competent workers, wrought incalculable injury to the strike everywhere, especially in the Youngstown district.

The Youngstown authorities, to begin with, were reasonably fair towards the strikers; but as the strike wore on and the steel companies and business men became desperate at the determined resistance of the workers, they began to apply " Pennsylvania tactics." In Youngstown and East Youngstown, Mayors Craver and McVey prohibited meetings, " the object of which is discussion of matters pertaining to prolonging the strike." [1] On November 22, district secretary McCadden, and organizers John Klinsky and Frank Kurowsky were arrested in East Youngstown, charged with criminal syndicalism and held for $3,000 bonds each. Later a whole local

[1] Youngstown *Vindicator*, November 24, 1919.

[176]

union, No. 104 Amalgamated Association, was arrested in the same town for holding a business meeting. " Citizens' committees " were formed, and open threats made to tar and feather all the organizers and drive them out of town. But the steel companies were unable to inflame public opinion sufficiently for them to venture this outrage.

Afterward the organizers were discharged; and in releasing the men arrested for holding a business meeting, Judge David G. Jenkins said:

> I regard the ordinance (E. Youngstown anti-free assembly) as a form of hysteria which has been sweeping the country, whereby well-meaning people, in the guise of patriots, have sought to preserve America even though going to the extent of denying the fundamental principles upon which Americanism is based, and free assemblage is one of those fundamentals.

In the principal outlying towns of the Youngstown district, namely Butler, Farrell, Sharon, Newcastle and Canton, the strikers were given the worst of it. The first four being Pennsylvania towns, no specific description of them is necessary. Suffice it to say that typical Cossack conditions prevailed. In Canton it was not much better. The companies turned loose many vicious gunmen on the strikers. The mayor was removed from office and his place given to a company man; and a sweeping injunction was issued against the strikers, denying them many fundamental rights.[1] The district, nevertheless, held remarkably well.

Cleveland from the first to the last was one of the

[1] No history of the movement in the Youngstown district could be complete without some mention of the assistance rendered the workers by Bishop John Podea of the Roumanian Greek Catholic church,

[177]

strong points in the battle line. On September 22 the men struck almost 100 per cent. in all the big plants, and until the very end preserved a wonderful solidarity. Under the excellent control of the organizers working with Secretary Raisse there was at no time a serious break in the ranks, and when the strike was called off on January 8, at least 50 per cent. of the men were still out, with production not over 30 per cent. of normal. Thousands of the men refused to go back to the mills at all, leaving them badly crippled.

The backbone of the Cleveland strike was the enormous mills of the American Steel and Wire Co. This calls attention to the fact that, as a whole, the employees of this subsidiary of the U. S. Steel Corporation made incomparably a better fight than did the workers in any other considerable branch of the steel industry. Long after the strike had been cracked in all other sections of the industry, the rod and wire mill men of Cleveland, Donora, Braddock, Rankin, Joliet and Waukegan stood practically solid. Even as late as December 27, only twelve days before the end, the companies were forced to the expedient of assembling a rump meeting in Cleveland of delegates from many centres, for the purpose of

Youngstown, and Rev. E. A. Kirby, pastor of St. Rose Roman Catholic church of Girard, Ohio. Usually the churchmen (of all faiths) in the various steel towns were careful not to jeopardize the fat company contributions by helping the unions. But not these men. They realized that all true followers of the Carpenter of Nazareth had to be on the side of the oppressed steel workers; and throughout the entire campaign they distinguished themselves by unstinted cooperation with the unions. The service was never too great nor the call too often for them to respond willingly.

calling off the strike. But the men voted unanimously for continuation under the leadership of the National Committee. When the strike was finally ended, however, they accepted the decision with good grace, because they were penetrated with the general strike idea and realized the folly of trying alone to whip the united steel companies.

The remarkable fight of the rod and wire mill men was due in large measure to the peculiar circumstances surrounding their organization. These are highly important and require explanation: The regular system used by the National Committee resulted usually in organization from the bottom upward; that is, in response to the general appeals made to the men in the great mass meetings, ordinarily the first to join the unions were the unskilled, who are the workers with the least to lose, the most to gain, and consequently those most likely to take a chance. Gradually, as the confidence of the men developed, the movement would extend on up through the plants until it included the highest skilled men. Given time and a reasonable opportunity, it was an infallible system. It was far superior to the old trade-union plan of working solely from the top down, because the latter always stopped before it got to the main body of the men, the unskilled workers.

The " bottom upward " system was used with the rod and wire mills, the same as with all others. But while it was operating the skilled men who had been attracted to the movement in Joliet, Donora and Cleveland started a " top downward " movement of their own. They sent committees to all the

[179]

large rod and wire mills in the country, appealing to the skilled men to organize. These committeemen, actual workers and acquainted with all the old timers in the business, could do more real organizing in a day with their tradesmen than regular organizers could in a month. Hardly would they go into a locality, no matter how difficult, than they would at once inspire that confidence in the movement which is so indispensible, and which takes organizers so long to develop. The result was a " top downward " movement working simultaneously with the " bottom upward " drive, which produced a high degree of organization for the rod and wire mill men.

A great weakness of the strike was the failure of many skilled workers to participate therein. This tended directly to aid the employers, and also to discourage the unskilled workers, who looked for their more expert brothers to take the lead in the strike as well as in the regular shop experiences. The explanation has been offered that this aloofness was because the skilled men are " unorganizable." But this is a dream. In the mills controlled by it, the Amalgamated Association (which is really a skilled workers' union) has thousands of them in its ranks, most of whom earn higher wages than employees of similar classes in the Trust mills. If the proper means to organize them could have been applied, the skilled workers would have been the leaders in the late strike, instead of generally the scabs. The same thing done in the rod and wire mills should have been done in all the important sections of the industry, blast furnaces, open hearths, sheet, tin, rail, plate, tube mills, etc. Committees of well-known skilled workers in these departments should have been sent forth everywhere to start movements from the top to meet the great surge coming up from the bottom. Had this been done, then Gary with all his millions could not have broken the strike. The tie-up would have been so complete and enduring that a settlement would have been compulsory.

But it was impossible; the chronic lack of resources prevented it. With the pitifully inadequate funds and men at its disposal, all the National Committee could do was to go ahead with its general campaign, leaving the detail and special work undone. It is certainly to be hoped that in the next big drive this committee system will be extensively followed. It is the solution of the skilled worker problem, and when applied intelligently in connection with the fundamental " bottom upward " movement, it must result in the organization of the industry.

In the Bethlehem Steel Company's plants the strike was not very effective. This was due principally to the failure of previous strikes and to general lack of organization. In Reading and in Lebanon there had been strikes on for many weeks before the big walkout. The workers' ranks there were already broken. In Sparrows' Point likewise several departments had been on strike since May 3. Not more than 500 men, principally laborers and tin mill workers, responded to the general strike call; but they made a hard fight of it. In Steelton the men had been very strongly organized during the war; but the error was made of putting all the trades

[181]

into one federal union. Then when the craft unions insisted later that their men be turned over to them, the resultant resistance of the members, and especially of the paid officers, virtually destroyed the organization. When the strike came only a small percentage struck, nor did they stick long.

Speaking of the strike in the main plant at Bethlehem, Secretary Hendricks says:

> The strike was called September 29, and about 75 per cent. of the men responded. These were largely American workers. The Machinists, which comprise about 40 per cent. of the total workers, were the craft most involved. In the mill and blast furnace departments, the response was among the rollers, heaters, and highly skilled men generally, which led to the complete shut-down of these departments. The molders practically shut the foundries down. Electrical workers, steamfitters, millwrights, and general repairmen responded well. The patternmakers did not go out.

The first break came a week later. It was charged largely to the steam engineers, who heeded the strike-breaking advice of their international officials and returned to work. Another factor was the failure of support from the railroad men on the inter-plant system. Had these two bodies of men been held in line by their officers, the Bethlehem strike would have been a success.

In the Bethlehem situation too much reliance was placed in the skilled trades; more attention should have been given to the organization of the real fighting force, the unskilled workers. Another mistake was to have allowed the strikes to take place in Reading, Lebanon and Sparrows' Point. Even a tyro could see that they had no hope of success. Those men could easily have been held in line until the big strike, to the enormous strengthening of the latter. The National Committee had little to do with the Bethlehem situation before the strike, the movement developing to a great extent independently.

Nowhere in the strike zone was there a more bitter fight than in the Buffalo district, which was directed by organizers Thompson and Streifler. All the important plants were affected, but the storm centered around the Lackawanna Steel Company. This concern left nothing undone to defeat its workers. For eight months it had prevented any meetings from being held in Lackawanna, and then, when the workers broke through this obstruction and crowded into the unions, it discharged hundreds of them. This put the iron into the workers' hearts, and they made an heroic struggle. So firm were their ranks that when the general strike was called off on January 8, they voted to continue the fight in Lackawanna. But this was soon seen to be hopeless.

Much company violence was used in the Lackawanna strike. The New York State Constabulary and the company guards, of a cut with their odious Pennsylvania brethren, slugged, shot and jailed men and women in real Steel Trust style. Many strikers were injured, and two killed outright. One of these, Joseph Mazurek, a native-born American, was freshly back from the fighting in France. Lackawanna was just a little bit of an industrial hell.[1]

[1] In connection with this matter it is interesting to note that

As a strike measure the Lackawanna Steel Company evicted many strikers from the company houses. In Braddock, Rankin, Homestead, Butler, Wierton, Natrona, Bethlehem and many other places, the companies put similar pressure upon their men, either evicting them or foreclosing the mortgages on their half-paid-for houses. Threats of such action drove thousands back to work, it being peculiarly terrifying to workers to find themselves deprived of their homes in winter time. Where evictions actually occurred the victims usually had to leave town or find crowded quarters with other strikers. The much-lauded housing schemes of the steel companies are merely one of a whole arsenal of weapons to crush the independence of their workers. No employer should be permitted to own or control the houses in which his men live.

The Wheeling district is noted as strong union country. The "independent" mills therein had provided the main strength of the Amalgamated Association for several years prior to this movement; but the Trust mills were still unorganized. Under the guidance of National Committee local secretary J. M. Peters, however, these men, in the mills of Wheeling, Bellaire, Benwood and Martin's Ferry, were brought into the unions. On September 22 they struck 100 per cent., completely closing all the plants. They held practically solid

after the strike had ended the union men entered suits against the steel companies for heavy damages. Up to the present writing the Lackawanna Steel Company, realizing the indefensibility of the outrages, has made out-of-court settlements to the extent of $22,500.

until the first week in December, when they broke heavily.

The immediate cause of this break merits explanation. The National Committee, at the outset of the strike, organized a publicity department, headed by Mr. Edwin Newdick, formerly of the National War Labor Board. In addition to getting out strike stories for the press, many of which were written by the well-known novelist, Mary Heaton Vorse, this department assembled and issued in printed bulletin form statistical information relative to the progress and effectiveness of the strike. The steel companies, through spies in the unions, newspapers, etc., disputed this information, telling the strikers that they were being victimized as the mills in all districts except their own were in full operation, and advising them to send out committees to investigate the situation.

It was a seductive argument and many were deceived by it. Consequently, quite generally, such committees (usually financed and chaperoned by the local Chambers of Commerce) went forth from various localities. Of course, they returned the sort of reports the companies wished. Much harm was done thereby. The Steubenville district suffered from the lying statement of such a committee, the strikers having made a winning fight up till the time it was made public, the middle of November. But nowhere was the effect so serious as in the Wheeling district.

The Wheeling committee was headed by one Robert Edwards, widely known for years as an extreme radical. It visited many points in the steel industry, taking its figures on steel production and strike conditions from employers' sources, and completely ignoring national and local strike officials everywhere. The ensuing report pictured the steel industry as virtually normal. Although he had been recently expelled from the Amalgamated Association Edwards still had great influence with the men, and his report broke their ranks. In future general strikes drastic disciplinary measures should be taken to forestall the activities of such committees.

Of the 6500 men employed by the Colorado Fuel and Iron Co. in its Pueblo mills, 95 per cent. walked out on September 22. When the strike was called off three and one-half months later not over 1500 of these had returned to their jobs. Production was below 20 per cent. of normal. Locally the tie-up was so effective that on January 9, at the biggest labor meeting in Pueblo's history, National Committee local secretary W. H. Young and the other organizers had to beg the men for hours to go back to work. These officials knew that the great struggle had been decided in the enormous steel centers of the East (Pueblo being credited with producing only two per cent. of the nation's steel) and that it would be madness for them to try to win the fight alone.

The heart of the Pueblo strike was opposition to the Rockefeller Industrial Plan, in force in the mills. This worthless, tyrannical arrangement the men could not tolerate and were determined to contest to the end. Realizing the minor importance of the Pueblo mills in the national strike, the men offered at the outset to waive all their demands pending its settlement, provided the company would agree to meet with their representatives later to take up these matters. But this was flatly refused; it was either accept the Rockefeller Plan or fight, even though 98 per cent. of the men had voted to abolish it.

Shortly after this incident John D. Rockefeller, Jr., gained much favorable comment and pleasing publicity by his glowing speech about industrial democracy and the right of collective bargaining, delivered at the National Industrial Conference at Washington, D. C. He was hailed as one of the country's progressive employers. But when the striking Pueblo workers wired him, requesting that he grant them these rights, he referred them to Mr. Welborn, President of the C. F. and I. Company, well knowing that this gentleman would deny their plea.

The strike was markedly peaceful throughout, no one being hurt and hardly any one arrested. But on December 28, the state militia were suddenly brought in, ostensibly because of an attack supposed to have been made two days previously upon Mr. F. E. Parks, manager of the Minnequa works. The public never learned the details of this mysterious affair which served so well to bring in the troops. Nor was the " culprit " ever located, although large rewards were offered for his capture.

The Johnstown strike was so complete that for eight weeks the great Cambria Steel Co., despite strenuous efforts, could not put a single department

of its enormous mills into operation. Every trick
was used to break the strike. The Back-To-Work
organization [1] labored ceaselessly, holding meetings
and writing and telephoning the workers to coax or
intimidate them back to their jobs. Droves of scabs
were brought in from outside points. But to no
effect; the workers held fast. Then the company
embarked upon the usual Pennsylvania policy of terrorism.

I, personally, was the first to feel its weight. I
was billed to speak in Johnstown on November 7.
Upon alighting from the train I was met by two
newspaper men who advised me to quit the town at
once, stating that the business men and company officials had held a meeting the night before and organized a " Citizens' Committee," which was to
break the strike by applying " Duquesne tactics."
Beginning with myself, all the organizers were to
be driven from the city. Disregarding this warning, I started for the Labor Temple; but was again
warned by the newspapermen, and finally stopped on
the street by city detectives, who told me that it
would be at the risk of my life to take a step nearer
the meeting place. I demanded protection, but it
was not forthcoming. I was told to leave.

In the meantime, Secretary Conboy arriving upon
the scene, the two of us started to the Mayor's office to protest, when suddenly, in broad daylight, at
a main street corner in the heart of the city, a mob

---

[1] These Back-To-Work organizations were formed in many steel
towns; their purpose was to recruit scabs. They were composed of
company officials, business men and " loyal " workers. The companies furnished the wherewithal to finance them.

STEEL TRUST NEWSPAPER PROPAGANDA

Pittsburgh *Chronicle Telegraph*, October 6, 1919.

of about forty men rushed us. Shouldering me away from Mr. Conboy, they stuck guns against my ribs and took me to the depot. While there they made a cowardly attempt to force me to sign a Back-To-Work card, which meant to write myself down a scab. Later I was put aboard an eastbound train. Several of the mob accompanied me to Conemaugh, a few miles out. The same night this "Citizens' Committee," with several hundred more, surrounded the organizers in their hotel and gave them twenty-four hours time to leave town. The city authorities refused to stir to defend them, and the following day organizers T. J. Conboy, Frank Hall, Frank Butterworth, and Frank Kurowsky were compelled to go. Domenick Gelotte, a local organizer of the miners, refused to depart and was promptly arrested. Up to this time the strike had been perfectly peaceful. The shut-down was so thorough that not even a picket line was necessary.

The mob perpetrating these outrages (duly praised by the newspapers as examples of 100 per cent. Americanism) was led by W. R. Lunk, secretary of the Y. M. C. A., and H. L. Tredennick, president of the chamber of commerce. This pair freely stated that the strike could never be broken by peaceful means, and that they were prepared to apply the necessary violence, which they did. Of course, they were never arrested. Had they been workers and engaged in a similar escapade against business men, they would have been lucky to get off with twenty years imprisonment apiece.

After a couple of weeks the organizers returned to Johnstown. Their efforts at holding the men together were so fruitful that the Cambria Company, in its own offices, organized a new mob to drive them out again. But this time, better prepared, they stood firm. On November 29, when the fresh deportation was to take place, Secretary Conboy demanded that Mayor Francke give him and the others protection. He offered to furnish the city a force of 1000 union ex-service men to preserve law and order. This offer was refused, and the Mayor and Sheriff reluctantly agreed to see that peace was kept. They informed the business men's mob that there was nothing doing. It was a tense situation. Had the threatened deportation been attempted, most serious trouble would surely have resulted.

In the meantime numbers of the State Constabulary had been sent into town (the city and county authorities denying responsibility for their presence) and they terrorized the workers in their customary, brutal way. Eventually the result sought by all this outlawry developed; a break occurred in the ranks of the highly-paid, skilled steel workers. Although small at first, the defection gradually spread as the weeks rolled on, until, by January 8, about two-thirds of the men had returned to work.

Considered nationally, strike sentiment continued strong until about the middle of the third month, when a feeling of pessimism regarding the outcome began to manifest itself among the various international organizations. Consequently, a meeting of the National Committee was held in Washington on December 13 and 14, to take stock of the situation. At this meeting I submitted the following figures:

District	Men on Strike Sept. 29	Men on Strike Dec. 10
Pittsburgh	25,000	8,000
Homestead	9,000	5,500
Braddock-Rankin	15,000	8,000
Clairton	4,000	1,500
Duquesne-McKeesport	12,000	1,000
Vandergrift	4,000	1,800
Natrona-Brackenridge	5,000	1,500
New Kensington	1,100	200
Apollo	1,500	200
Leechburg	3,000	300
Donora-Monessen	12,000	10,000
Johnstown	18,000	7,000
Coatesville	4,000	500
Youngstown district	70,000	12,800
Wheeling district	15,000	3,000
Cleveland	25,000	15,000
Steubenville district	12,000	2,000
Chicago district	90,000	18,000
Buffalo	12,000	5,000
Pueblo	6,000	5,000
Birmingham	2,000	500
Bethlehem Plants (5)	20,000	2,500
	365,600	109,300

Estimated production of steel, 50 to 60 per cent. of normal capacity.

Owing to the chaotic conditions in many steel districts, it was exceedingly difficult at all times to get accurate statistics upon the actual state of affairs. Those above represented the very best that the National Committee's whole organizing force could assemble. The officials of the Amalgamated Association strongly favored calling off the strike, but agreed that the figures cited on the number of men still out were conservative and within the mark. The opinion prevailed that the strike was still effective and that it should be vigorously continued.

On January 3 and 4, the National Committee met in Pittsburgh. At this gathering it soon became evident that the strike was deemed hopeless, so, according to its custom when important decisions had to be made, the National Committee called a special meeting for January 8, all the international organizations being notified. The situation was bad. Reliable reports on January 8 showed the steel companies generally to have working forces of from 70 to 80 per cent., and steel production of from 60 to 70 per cent. of normal. Possibly 100,000 men still held out; but it seemed merely punishing these game fighters to continue the strike. They were being injured by it far more than was the Steel Trust. There was no hope of a settlement, the steel companies being plainly determined now to fight on indefinitely. Therefore, in justice to the loyal strikers and to enable them to go back to the mills with clear records, the meeting adopted, by a vote of ten unions to five, a sub-committee's report providing that the strike be called off; that the commissaries be closed as fast as conditions in the various localities would permit, and that the campaign of education and organization of the steel workers be continued with undiminished vigor.

At this point, wishing to have the new phase of the work go ahead with a clean slate, I resigned my office as Secretary-Treasurer of the National Committee. Mr. J. G. Brown was elected to fill the vacancy. The following telegram was sent to all the strike centers, and given to the press:

The Steel Corporations, with the active assistance of

the press, the courts, the federal troops, state police, and many public officials, have denied steel workers their rights of free speech, free assembly and the right to organize, and by this arbitrary and ruthless misuse of power have brought about a condition which has compelled the National Committee for Organizing Iron and Steel Workers to vote today that the active strike phase of the steel campaign is now at an end.   A vigorous campaign of education and re-organization will be immediately begun and will not cease until industrial justice has been achieved in the steel industry.   All steel strikers are now at liberty to return to work pending preparations for the next big organization movement.

John Fitzpatrick,
D. J. Davis,
Edw. J. Evans,
Wm. Hannon,
Wm. Z. Foster.

The great steel strike was ended.

XI

NATIONAL AND RACIAL ELEMENTS

A MODERN BABEL — AMERICANS AS SKILLED WORKERS — FOREIGNERS AS UNSKILLED WORKERS — LANGUAGE DIFFICULTIES — THE NEGRO IN THE STRIKE — THE RACE PROBLEM

IN order to prove its charge that the purpose of the steel strike was contrary to the spirit of our institutions, the Steel Trust's great propaganda organization never ceased asserting, (1) that the strike was a movement of foreigners, (2) that the Americans in the mills were opposed to it for patriotic reasons and were taking no part therein. The vicious press made much capital of these allegations, using them heavily against the strike. Now let us see how much truth there was in them:

1. Unquestionably the foreign-born were in the majority among the strikers; but how could it be otherwise in view of the fact that they make up the bulk of the working force in the industry? The following table, submitted to the Senate Committee by Mr. A. F. Diehl, General Manager of the Duquesne Works of the Carnegie Steel Co., illustrates this fact: [1]

[1] Senate Committee Steel Strike Hearings, page 532.

RECAPITULATION OF NATIONALITIES, AS OF AUG. 1ST, 1919, FOR TOTAL PLANT, DUQUESNE WORKS

Nationality	Total	Per cent.
American	2,097	34.6
American (colored)	344	5.7
English	147	2.4
Scotch	41	.7
Welsh	28	.5
Irish	58	.9
Canadian	4	.1
German	104	1.8
French	6	.1
Swedish	79	1.3
Italian	128	2.1
Greek	23	.4
Swiss	5	.1
Norwegian	4	.1
Danish	1	.0
Hollander	1	.0
Russian	185	3.0
Lithuanian	201	3.3
Lattis	3	.0
Bohemian	3	.0
Croatian	222	3.7
Magyar	742	12.2
Slovak	930	15.3
Roumanian	7	.1
Ruthenian	82	1.3
Bulgarian	25	.4
Servian	219	3.6
Polish	246	4.0
Armenian	34	.5
Dalmatian	6	.1
Macedonian	10	.2
Hebrew	10	.2
Turkish	80	1.3
Totals	6,075	100.00

This condition is typical of steel mills generally in the greater Pittsburgh and Middle West districts, where the body of the industry is located. In Clairton, of 4,600 employees, divided into 39 nationalities, 35 per cent. are Americans. On page 480 of the report of the Senate Committee Steel Strike Hearings, appears a table covering the employees of the Homestead Steel Works, Howard Axle Works, and Carrie Furnaces (an industrial unit), submitted by General Manager J. S. Oursler. It shows a total of 14,687 employees, of 54 nationality divisions. Of these employees, 5,799, or 39.45 per cent. are stated to be American whites. But as Mr. Oursler re-iterated in his testimony that he had classed as Americans all those who had their citizenship papers, both these figures should therefore be considerably reduced. Besides, it must be borne in mind that these several tables include the office forces, bosses, etc., which are almost entirely American, and which were not involved in the strike. In the steel districts in question it is exceedingly doubtful if over 25 per cent. of the actual workers are American-born whites. How, then, can a general strike of steel workers be anything else than largely a strike of foreigners?

2. Regarding the alleged non-participation of Americans in the movement: Although in many districts where the strike was practically 100 per cent. effective, the Americans struck almost to a man with the other workers and fought gamely to the finish, nevertheless it must be admitted that in the main, when compared with the foreigners,[1] they made a

[1] In steel industry usage (followed in this book unless otherwise noted) the term "foreigners" applies chiefly to the nationalities of the later immigrations, including the Slavic races, Roumanians,

[196]

poor showing. To begin with they organized slowly; then they struck reluctantly and scatteringly; and finally, they showed little tenacity as strikers. But this general sluggishness originated, however, not in patriotic objections to the movement or lack of sympathy with its aims; but chiefly because the Americans, as skilled workers, were naturally slower and less determined in action than the foreigners, or unskilled workers.

In the steel industry the most skilled men are to be found in those trades actually engaged in the making and rolling of iron and steel — the melters, puddlers, shearmen, rollers, roughers, heaters, Bessemer blowers, etc. These men are paid upon a tonnage basis and generally receive considerably higher wages than the mechanical tradesmen — bricklayers, machinists, boilermakers, riggers, firemen, engineers, electrical workers, blacksmiths, etc., who build, maintain and generally operate the plants. It is among the favored tonnage trades that the Americans are especially intrenched.

In the old days these highly skilled workers took the initiative in the struggle for human rights in the steel industry — the mechanical trades and unskilled workers playing a very minor part. Homestead was one of their great battles, only 752 of the 3800 men employed being union members in good-standing. They were then bold, militant and tenacious as

Bulgarians, Hungarians, Greeks, Italians and others from Eastern and Southern Europe. These are the so-called "hunkies." The peoples of the earlier immigrations — the English, Irish, Scotch, Welsh, Germans and Scandinavians — who speak our language, hold good jobs, and are generally well established, are not exactly considered Americans, but they are rarely called foreigners.

[197]

bull dogs. But since those times they have been defeated so often, due to a weakening of their proportional strength and strategical position, that they have lost much of the independent spirit which once characterized them. They now fear the power of the Steel Trust; they dread its pitiless blacklist; they hesitate to put in jeopardy their comparatively good jobs, which they secured only after long years of service in minor positions, and which, once lost, are so hard to regain. They want better conditions now as much as they ever did, but they lack the self-confidence to fight for them. All through the campaign their attitude, barring the exceptions here and there, was to wait until the lesser skilled men had so far perfected the organization as to make it seem safe for them to join it. When the strike came the unskilled workers led the way; then came the mechanical trades; with the aristocratic steel workers bringing up the rear. But in scurrying back to scab in the mills, the order was just the reverse. This was the experience in virtually every section of the industry.

It would be wrong, however, to say that the failure of American workers to participate more heartily in the movement was due solely to their favored position in the industry. To some extent race prejudice also came into play, especially in those districts where the organization had not yet reached far enough up into the plants to include the skilled workers. Everywhere American-born workingmen, unfortunately, are prone to look with some suspicion, if not contempt and hatred, upon foreigners, whom they have been taught to believe are injuring their standard of living. The companies made the most of this. Dubbing the walkout a " hunky " strike, they told the Americans that if it succeeded the latter would have to give over to the despised foreigners all the good jobs and shop privileges they enjoyed. Their slogan was " Don't let the ' hunkies ' rule the mills." They openly circulated handbills inciting to race war. The following, from Elwood, Pa., where a National Tube Company plant is located, is typical:

WAKE UP AMERICANS!!

ITALIAN LABORERS, organized under the American Federation of Labor are going to strike Monday and are threatening workmen who want to continue working.

These foreigners have been told by labor agitators that if they would join the union they would get Americans' jobs.

They are being encouraged by ITALIAN MER-CHANTS, who are in sympathy with them.

ARE YOU GOING TO SLEEP AND LET MOB RULE THREATEN THE PEACE OF OUR TOWN?

In towns where often the foreign population is three-fourths of the whole, such propaganda was most inflammatory. The newspapers did all they could to make it more so. They solemnly warned of the danger of a foreign uprising and advised a campaign of militant, 100 per cent. Americanism; which meant, on the one hand for the local authorities, gunmen, and business men to set up a reign of terror, and on the other, for the workers all to go back to work at once. The courts and so-called peace officers did their part. They jailed, clubbed and shot the foreigners and left the Americans, even if they were strikers, in comparative immunity. Nothing was left undone to create a race issue, and it is not surprising that many American workers, unorganized and ignorant, were mislead by this and inveigled back to the mills.

It has been charged that the unions neglected the American steel workers and concentrated upon the organization of the foreigners. If anything, the reverse is true; for by far the weight of the appeal made was to the English speaking elements. Every piece of literature put out stressed heavily the English language. Of twenty-five National Committee district and local secretaries, only three were born in Europe; of a dozen Amalgamated Association organizers, not one spoke anything but English, and of the crew as a whole, over 80 per cent. were American born. By its very nature such an organizing force had to make strong appeal to the American workers. In fact, the foreigners constantly insisted upon this, because, strangers in a strange land, they always crave and seek American co-operation in their union movements. That this co-operation was not more in evidence in the steel campaign was the cause of much bitter complaint among them.

But if the Americans and skilled workers generally proved indifferent union men in the steel campaign, the foreign, unskilled workers covered themselves with glory. Throughout the whole affair they showed an understanding discipline, courage and tenacity of purpose that compared favorably with that shown in any organized effort ever put forth by workingmen on this continent. Beyond question they displayed trade-union qualities of the very highest type. Their solidarity was unbreakable; their fighting spirit invincible. They nobly struggled onward in the face of difficulties that would try the stoutest hearts. They proved themselves altogether worthy of the best American labor traditions. Thousands of them were intending to return to Europe shortly and apparently had slight reason to establish good conditions here; but they fought on, many spending their little savings during the strike, and thus postponing indefinitely the long-looked-for trip to the homelands.

This attitude of the foreign workers is a bitter pill for the Steel Trust. For many years it had scoured the countries of Eastern and Southern Europe, and packed its mills with poor, dispirited, ignorant immigrants of three score nationalities, in the hope that it was finally supplanting its original crew of independent American and Western European workmen by a race of submissive, unorganizable slaves. And for a long time this shameful policy worked well. Wages sank to nowhere; conditions became unspeakably wretched; every strike of the old-time, organized workers was smothered by an avalanche of job-hungry immigrants.[1] But now

[1] The brazen frankness with which this policy was carried out is illustrated by the following advertisement, which appeared in the Pittsburgh *Gazette-Times,* July 15, 1909, during the big steel strike of that time:

MEN WANTED — Tinners, catchers and helpers to work in open shops. Syrians, Poles and Roumanians preferred. Steady employment and good wages to men willing to work. Fare paid and no fees charged.

these foreigners are waking up; in consequence of hard economic conditions, a better acquaintance with our language and institutions, an inherent class solidarity, the example of union men in other industries, and the social upheavals in Europe, these men are opening their eyes; and they are fast taking their place in the very front rank of the working class fighters for industrial liberty. And now the Steel Trust, discovering that its hoped-for-scabs are in truth highly rebellious workingmen, is making the welkin ring with inconsistent denunciation of the " revolutionary foreigners," with whom just a short while ago it was so anxious to crowd its plants. The biter has been very badly bitten.

For the unions the nationality problem was serious throughout the entire campaign — the employers had worked for years to make it an insoluble one. Something of the situation may be gleaned when it is recalled that the steel industry comprises hundreds of mills, scattered through a dozen states, and employing half a million workers. These speak dozens of widely differing languages, worship through many mutually antagonistic religions, and are moved by numberless racial and national animosities. Yet the National Committee, with the skimped resources it had in hand, had to and did weld together this vast polyglot, heterogeneous mass into a voluntary organization, kept it thinking alike, and held it in strong discipline for months in the face of the bitter opposition of the Steel Trust, which sought in every conceivable way to divide the workers by playing upon their multiplicity of fears and prejudices.

In accomplishing this huge task the first requisite

was to overcome the language difficulty sufficiently to permit the message of trade unionism to be brought forcefully to the many diverse elements. Because doing so would have rendered the meetings ruinously cumbersome and unwieldy, it was out of the question to utilize all the languages or any considerable number of them; so the plan was followed of using only the predominant ones; the theory being that if the large bodies of workers speaking them could be reached, they in turn would find means to influence the minorities speaking other languages.

As the various foreign groups tend strongly to colonize in certain districts, the basic languages spoken in a given plant, regardless of how many nationalities work therein, ordinarily number not more than four or five, including always English, usually a couple of the Slavic tongues (Slavish, Polish, Russian, Croatian, Lithuanian, Serbian, etc.), often Hungarian, and occasionally Italian, Roumanian or Greek. For example, among the fifty-four nationalities in the big Homestead plants, the principal languages spoken are, in the order of their numerical importance, English, Slavish, Russian, Hungarian and Polish. Move these predominate language groups and you move the whole working force; that was the system in the steel campaign. Seldom was a piece of literature issued, even for national circulation, with as many as six languages upon it; the vitally important strike call had but seven, while four was the customary number.

About twenty-five organizers who spoke these predominating languages were put in the field. Great care was taken by the A. F. of L., National Committee and co-operating unions to select reliable, level-headed men of influence and standing among their respective peoples, men who could be depended upon to go along with the general program, and not to work upon some destructive side-issue of their own. Besides, efforts were made to take every possible advantage of the fact that practically all the foreign workers have some slight smattering of English. Accordingly, the English-speaking organizers were coached to get rid of all trade-union technical expressions and to confine their talks to fundamentals; to speak slowly, distinctly, and in the simplest, even " pidjinized " terms, to illustrate the whole with sign language, and to follow out a system of repetition and restatement that was bound to make their meaning plain to the most unknowing. Such talks, while not calculated to stir the emotions, made clear the situation and were greatly appreciated by the foreigners, thousands of whom, during the steel campaign, for the first time felt the pleasure and encouragement of understanding the despairingly difficult English spoken from a platform. The steel workers' meetings were schools in practical Americanization.[1]

With the language problem solved in even this imperfect way, the persistent advocacy of labor union principles, backed up by a few thoroughgoing, com-

[1] During the great organization drive in the Chicago packing houses in 1917–18, this method was used for several months in the large local union of car builders and repairmen, fully 90 per cent. of whom, born in Eastern Europe, were supposedly non-English-speaking. As a result they acquired such confidence in their ability to use the language that they dropped the customary practice of translating all their business into several languages and took to using English only.

mon-sense systems of organization, did the rest. Gradually the great armies of linguistically, religiously, racially divided steel workers were united into the mighty force which threw itself against the Steel Trust. In the main the foreign workers were simple, sincere, earnest minded folk, naturally disposed to co-operative effort. While the individualistic, sophisticated American workers all too often attended the ball games and filled the pool rooms, the foreigners packed the union meeting halls. Their worst fault was a woeful unacquaintance with trade-union methods. This the organizers diligently labored to overcome by patient instruction and a faithful attendance to their duties. The general result was that the foreign workers developed a confidence in the organizers and a loyalty to the unions, which not even the heavy shock of the loss of the strike has been able to destroy.

The indifference, verging often into open hostility, with which negroes generally regard Organized Labor's activities, manifested itself strongly in the steel campaign. Those employed in the industry were extremely resistent to the trade-union program; those on the outside allowed themselves to be used freely as strike-breakers.

According to the Immigration Commission's Report, which furnished the latest official figures (period 1907–08), 4.7 per cent. of the total number of steel industry employees at that time were negroes, most of whom were located in the Alabama and Maryland districts. Since then, however, considerable additions to their numbers have been made, and in many northern mills will be found groups of them, ranging in strength from 1 to 20 per cent. of the whole working force. They work mostly at hard, rough, unskilled labor, especially in the blast furnace department.

Generally speaking, these bodies of negroes took small part in the movement. In certain districts, notably Cleveland and Wheeling, it is true that they organized 100 per cent. and struck very creditably; but in most places, and exactly those where their support was needed the worst, they made a wretched showing. Consider the situation, for instance, in the Homestead Steel Works. In these plants (including the Carrie Furnaces at Rankin), of the 14,687 employees, 1,737 are negroes. Making deductions for office forces, bosses, etc., this would make them from 12 to 14 per cent. of the actual workers, a most important factor indeed. During the organizing campaign, of all these men, only eight joined the unions. And of these but one struck. He, however, stayed loyally to the finish. The degree of this abstention from the movement may be gauged when it is recalled that of the white unskilled workers in the same plants at least 75 per cent. joined the unions, and 90 per cent. struck.

Throughout the immediate Pittsburgh district, where the unions operated under such great handicaps and had to rely so much on the initiative of the individual workers, the same condition prevailed. In Duquesne, of 344 negroes employed, not one struck; in Clairton, of 300, six joined the unions and struck for two weeks. Of the several hundred working in the Braddock plants, not one joined a union or went on strike; and a dozen would cover those from the large number employed in the mills in Pittsburgh proper who walked out with the 25,000 whites on September 22. Similar tendencies were shown in the Chicago, Youngstown, Buffalo, Pueblo, Sparrows' Point and other districts. In the entire steel industry, the negroes, beyond compare, gave the movement less co-operation than any other element, skilled or unskilled, foreign or native.

Those on the outside of the industry seemed equally unsympathetic. National Committee secretaries' reports indicate that the Steel Trust recruited and shipped from 30,000 to 40,000 negroes into the mills as strike-breakers. Many of these were picked up in Northern cities, but the most of them came from the South. They were used in all the large districts and were a big factor in breaking the strike. The following statement illustrates some of the methods used in securing and handling them:

Monessen, November 23, 1919
Eugene Steward — Age 19 — Baltimore, Md.
My native place is Charleston, South Carolina.
I arrived in Monessen on Wednesday, November 19. There were about 200 of us loaded in the cars at Baltimore; some were white; and when we were loaded in the cars were told that we were being taken to Philadelphia.

We were not told that a strike was in progress. We were promised $4.00 a day, with the understanding that we should be boarded at $1.00 a day.

When we took the train a guard locked the doors so that we were unable to get out, and no meals were given us on the way, although we were promised board.

We were unloaded at Lock 4 and had a guard placed over us, and were then marched into the grounds of the Pittsburgh Steel Products Co. We were then told to go to work, and when I found out that there was a strike on I got out. They refused to let me out at the gate when I protested about working, and I climbed over the fence, and they caught me and compelled me to go back and sign a paper and told me that I would have to go to work. I told them that I would not go to work if they kept me there two years. I was placed on a boat. There were about 200 other people there. The guards informed me that if I made any attempt to again run away that they would shoot me. I got a rope and escaped, as I will not work to break the strike.

his
Eugene   X   Steward
mark

Witness Jacob S. McGinley

Few, however, of the imported negro strike-breakers showed the splendid spirit of this unlettered boy. Most of them seemed to take a keen delight in stealing the white men's jobs and crushing their strike. They clashed badly with the pickets, where picketing was allowed. And between them and the white strike-breakers many murderous encounters occurred in the mills, although the companies were very careful to suppress news of these outbreaks.

So serious was the race situation in the steel strike that the National Committee for Organizing Iron and Steel Workers requested President Gompers to arrange a conference between prominent negro leaders and trade-union officials, to the end that the proper remedies may be indicated. The need for action looking towards better relations between whites and blacks in the industrial field should be instantly patent; for there can be no doubt but that the employing class, taking advantage of the bitter animosities of the two groups, are deliberately attempting to turn the negroes into a race of strike-breakers, with whom to hold the white workers in check; on much the same principle as the Czars used the Cossacks to keep in subjection the balance of the Russian people. Should they succeed to any degree it would make our industrial disputes take on more and more the character of race wars, a consummation that would be highly injurious to the white workers and eventually ruinous to the blacks.

For the tense situation existing the unions are themselves in no small part to blame. Many of them sharply draw the color line, thus feeding the flames of race hatred. This discriminatory practice is in direct conflict with the fundamental which demands that all the workers be organized, without regard to sex, race, creed, politics or nationality. It injures Labor's cause greatly. Company agents harp upon it continually, to prevent negroes from joining even the organizations willing to take them in. This was the case in the steel compaign. Moreover these same company agents cited this discriminatory practice most effectively to induce thousands of outside colored workers to come into the industry as strike-breakers. Such a condition cannot be allowed to persist. But to relieve it the unions will have to meet the issue honestly and broad-mindedly. They must open their ranks to negroes, make an

[209]

earnest effort to organize them, and then give them a square deal when they do join. Nothing short of this will accomplish the desired result.[1]

This action by the unions will be a step in the right direction, but it alone will not solve the vexed problem. The best negro leaders must join heartily in destroying the pernicious anti-union policies so deeply rooted among their people. It is a lamentable fact, well known to all organizers who have worked in industries employing considerable numbers of negroes, that there is a large and influential black leadership, including ministers, politicians, editors, doctors, lawyers, social workers, etc., who as a matter of race tactics are violently opposed to their people going into the trade unions. They look upon strike-breaking as a legitimate and effective means of negro advancement. Time and again, they have seen their people, by use of it, readily work their way into trades and industries previously firmly sealed against them by the white workers' and white employers' prejudices. Nor can they see any wrong in thus taking advantage of the white man, who has so brutally oppressed them for centuries. On the contrary, they consider it a justified retaliation. They are in a race war. Inasmuch as the steel strike resulted in more negroes being in the industry than was the case before, they look upon the outcome as a victory. For these elements, and they are numerous and powerful among negroes, the color

[1] The Miners, Building Laborers and several other unions are taking the lead in this direction and are getting good results. Negroes are joining their ranks in considerable numbers and are proving themselves to be excellent union men.

line clauses in the union constitutions are meat and drink; such leaders don't want them abolished,— they make too strong an argument against the unions.

Consider the situation faced by the unions in the campaign to organize the Chicago packing houses in 1917–18. The negroes in this industry are a strong factor (numbering 14,000 of a total of some 65,000 employees), and the unions were determined to organize them. But no sooner had organizers begun the work than they met the firm opposition of the negro intelligencia above-noted. These warned their people to have nothing to do with the movement, as their interest lay in working with the packers to defeat the unions. They said that was how the negroes came into the packing industry, and that was how they would progress in it.

Naturally, they repeated the accusations about white men not taking negroes in their unions, a charge which was not true in the packing industry. The organizers replied by launching a vigorous campaign to get them into the unions. Then the propaganda was sent forth that the only reason the whites were willing to take the blacks into their locals was because the latter, being in a minority, could exert no control; that the whites would not dare to give them a local of their own, etc. This was met by the establishment of a negro local of miscellaneous workers in a convenient neighborhood. Then the Jim Crow cry was raised that the whites wanted the blacks to herd by themselves. This the organizers answered by insisting that a free transfer system be kept up between the white and black locals.

These were affiliated with the basic organization of the industry, the Amalgamated Meat Cutters and Butcher Workmen of North America.

But even this did not satisfy; the anti-union propaganda went on undiminished and with tremendous effect. It is true that some far-sighted negro intellectuals defended the unions; but they were as men crying in the wilderness; the others prevailed. And although the unions kept a crew of negro organizers in the field, and won many concessions for the packing house workers, including the eight hour day, right of collective bargaining, large increases in wages, 40 hour weekly guarantee, retro-active pay, seniority rights, etc., they have never succeeded in organizing the negroes.

They know little of the race problem in industry who declare that it can be settled merely by the unions opening their doors to the negroes. It is much more complex than that, and will require the best thought that conscientious whites and blacks can give it. The negro has the more difficult part to solve, in resisting the insidious efforts of unscrupulous white employers and misguided intellectuals of his own race to make a professional strike-breaker of him. But I am confident that he will win out and will take his place where he belongs in the industrial fight, side by side with the white worker.

XII

THE COMMISSARIAT — THE STRIKE
COST

THE RELIEF ORGANIZATION — RATIONS — SYSTEM
OF DISTRIBUTION — COST OF COMMISSARIAT —
STEEL STRIKE RELIEF FUND — COST OF THE
STRIKE TO THE WORKERS, THE EMPLOYERS, THE
PUBLIC, THE LABOR MOVEMENT

IN all strikes the problem of keeping the wolf from
the door is a pressing one. Usually it is met by the
unions involved paying regular benefits of from $5.00
to $15.00 per week to each striker. But in the steel
strike this was out of the question.[1] The tremendous number of men on strike and the scanty funds
available utterly forbade it. To have paid such
benefits would have required the impossible sum of
at least $2,000,000 per week. Therefore, the best
that could be done was to assist those families on the
brink of destitution by furnishing them free that
most basic of human necessities, food. Ordinarily
in strikes the main body of men are able to take care
of themselves over an extended period. The

[1] Exceptions to this were the cases of the Molders' and Coopers'
Unions. These organizations were compelled by constitutional re-
quirements to pay regular strike benefits. But they included only a
very small percentage of the total number of strikers.

[213]

danger point is in the poverty-stricken minority. From them come the hunger-driven scabs who so demoralize and discourage the men still out. Hence, to take care of this weaker element was scientifically to strengthen the steel strike, and to make the best use of the resources available.

The great mass of strikers and their incomplete organization making it manifestly impossible for each union to segregate and take care of its own members, the internationals affiliated with the National Committee (with the two exceptions noted) pooled their strike funds and formed a joint commissariat.[1] They then proceeded to extend relief to all needy strikers, regardless of their trades or callings, or even membership or non-membership in the unions. To get relief all that was necessary was to be a steel striker and in want. This splendid solidarity and rapid modification of trade-union tactics and institutions to meet an emergency is probably without a parallel in American labor annals.

The commissariat was entirely under the supervision and direction of the National Committee. Its national headquarters was in Pittsburgh, with a sub-district in Chicago. Goods were shipped from these two points. In Pittsburgh they were bought and handled through the Tri-State Co-operative Association, with National Committee employees making up the shipments. In Chicago the same was done through the National Co-operative Association. As Bethlehem, Birmingham, Pueblo and a few other

[1] The commissariat was suggested by John Fitzpatrick, as a result of his experiences in the Chicago Garment Workers' strike of a decade ago.

strike-bound towns lay beyond convenient shipping distance from the two distributing points, the men in charge there were sent checks and they bought their supplies locally.

The General Director of the commissariat was Robert McKechan, business manager of the Central States Wholesale Co-operative Association. He was paid by the Illinois Miners, District No. 2. He was ably assisted by A. V. Craig (Ass't. Director), Enoch Martin (Auditor — also paid by Illinois miners), Wm. Orr (Warehouse Manager), and E. G. Craig. Secretary De Young was in charge of the Chicago sub-district. The local distributing centres were operated altogether by National Committee local secretaries and volunteer strike committees, with an occasional paid assistant.

All told, 45 local commissaries were set up throughout the strike zone. This elaborate organization was created and put in motion almost over night. Within a week after Mr. McKechan arrived in Pittsburgh, he and officials of the National Committee had devised the commissary system — with hardly a precedent to go by,— organized its nation-wide machinery, and started the first shipment *en route* to the many strike centres. To break in this machinery, a small pro rata of provisions, based upon the number of men on strike, was sent to each place. The following week this was doubled, and each succeeding week it was increased to keep pace with the growing need. It finally developed into a huge affair. Few strikers had to be turned away for lack of food, and these only for a short while until the necessary additional stuff could be secured from the shipping points. Throughout the fourteen weeks it was in operation the commissariat, despite the tremendous difficulties it had to contend with, worked with remarkable smoothness. It was one of the greatest achievements of the entire steel campaign.

The wide extent of the relief work made it necessary to develop the most rigid simplicity and standardization in the apportionment of food to the strikers. Hence, only two sizes of rations could be used; one for families of five or less, and the other for families of six or more. These were varied from time to time, always bearing in mind the cooking facilities of the strikers and the many food likes and dislikes of the various nationalities. To facilitate the carrying away of the food and to make it last the better, two commissary days were held each week, in each locality. The rations were listed on large posters (white for families of five or less, and green for families of six or more) which were prominently displayed in the local commissaries in order that the strikers could see exactly how much provisions they were entitled to. The following are typical rations:

FAMILIES OF FIVE OR LESS

First Half Week		Second Half Week	
Potatoes	15 lbs.	Bread	4 loaves
Bread	4 loaves	Tomatoes	1 can
Tomatoes	1 can	Corn	1 "
Peas	1 "	Peas	1 "
Navy beans	4 lbs.	Red beans	4 lbs.
Oatmeal	1 box	Kraut	2 cans
Bacon	1 lb.	Dry salt meat	1 lb.
Coffee	1 "	Syrup	1 can
Milk	1 can		

JOHN FITZPATRICK
Chairman, National Committee for Organizing Iron and Steel Workers.

FAMILIES OF SIX OR MORE

First Half Week		Second Half Week	
Potatoes	10 lbs.	Potatoes	10 lbs.
Bread	5 loaves	Bread	5 loaves
Tomatoes	1 can	Tomatoes	1 can
Corn	1 "	Corn	1 "
Peas	1 "	Peas	1 "
Navy beans	5 lbs.	Kraut	2 cans
Oatmeal	2 boxes	Red beans	5 lbs.
Bacon	1 lb.	Dry salt meat	1 lb.
Coffee	1 "	Milk	1 can
Milk	1 can	Syrup	1 "

It was not contended that these rations were enough to sustain completely the recipients' families; but they helped mightily. Few, if any, went hungry. Single men in need received a half week's rations to last the week. The greatest care was taken to have the supplies of the best quality and in good condition. Whatever the unions gave they wanted the strikers to understand was in the best spirit of brotherly solidarity.[1]

The provisions were distributed strictly according to the following card system:

1. Identification card: An applicant requesting relief would be referred to a credentialed volunteer relief committee. If this committee deemed the case a needy one, it would issue the striker an identification card. This he was required to show when dealing at the commissary.

[1] In addition to the regular commissaries, the local organizations, grace to their own funds or occasional donations from their international unions, had relief enterprises of various sorts, such as soup kitchens, milk, clothes, rent and sickness funds. In Monessen and Donora the strikers actually served a big turkey dinner on Thanksgiving Day. Strikers paid five cents a plate for all they wished to eat. Sympathizers donated liberally according to their means. But the commissary system was the main source of strike relief.

2. Record card: In addition, the relief committee would write out the data of the case upon a record card and turn it over to the local secretary in charge of the commissary, who would keep it on file.

3. Commissary card: When the applicant presented his identification card at the commissary, the local secretary, referring to the record card on file, would make him out a commissary card, white or green, accordingly as his family was of five or less, or six or more members. This commissary card entitled him to draw supplies.

The commissary card had a stub attached. When a striker got his first half week's supplies, this stub would be detached and retained by the commissary clerk. Upon his next visit the body of the card would be taken up. Two important purposes were served by this collection of the commissary cards — rather than having permanent cards and merely punching them. First, the canceled cards being sent to the commissariat national headquarters, it proved conclusively that the strikers had actually received the provisions shipped to the district; and second, by compelling the strikers to get new commissary cards each week, it enabled the local secretaries to keep in close touch with those on the relief roll.

To lighten the load upon the many inexperienced men working in the various commissaries, a special effort was made to do as much of the technical work as possible in the main offices of the National Committee. Otherwise the commissariat could not possibly have succeeded. This consideration was a prime factor in restricting the buying of provisions to Pittsburgh, Chicago and the fewest practical number of outlying points. It also caused the adoption of the package system, all bulk goods, except potatoes, being prepared for delivery before leaving the warehouses. Likewise, the local bookkeeping was simplified to the last degree. In fact, for the most part the secretaries in charge of the commissaries hardly needed books at all. The whole system checked itself from the central points.

As an example of its working, let us suppose that the allotment of a certain town was 1000 rations. Accordingly, there would be shipped to that place exactly enough of each article to precisely cover the allotted number of rations. Then, if the secretary simply saw to it that he got what he was charged with and issued his supplies carefully in the right proportions, the whole transaction would balance to a pound, with hardly a scratch of a pen from him. The bookkeeping was all done at the general offices. The latter's assurances that each striker had received his proper ration and that the right number of rations had been issued were, in the first place, the ration posters hanging on the walls of the commissary; and in the second, the returned canceled commissary cards. Barring an occasional slight disruption from delayed shipments, spoiled goods, shortages, and a little carelessness here and there, the system worked very well.

The commissariat was in operation from October 26 until January 31, three weeks after the strike had ended. It was continued through this extra period in order to help to their feet the destitute strikers who had fought so nobly. Probably nothing done by the unions in the entire campaign won them so much good will with the steel workers as this one act.

The total cost of operating the commissariat was $348,509.42. The significance of this figure stands out when it is reduced to a per man basis. At the strike's start there were 365,600 men out, and at its finish about 100,000. Considering that few serious breaks occurred until the eighth to tenth weeks, a fair average for the whole period would be about 250,-000. Accordingly, this would give (disregarding the three weeks after January 8) a total relief cost of a fraction less than $1.40 per man for the entire fifteen weeks of the strike, or about one day's strike benefits of an ordinary union. Reduced to a weekly basis, it amounts to but $9\frac{1}{3}$ cents for each striker. Just how unusually small this sum is may be judged from the fact that the International Molders' Union paid the few men it had on strike regular benefits of $9.00 per week after the first week. The fact is that, except for a small, impoverished minority, the steel workers made their long, hard fight virtually upon their own resources.[1]

To help finance the commissariat the American Federation of Labor was requested to issue a general appeal for funds, which it did. Then, to add force to this call, the National Committee recruited and put in the field a corps of solicitors, including among others, Anton Johannson, J. D. Cannon,

[1] It is true, as noted above, that several other unions besides the Molders and Coopers made occasional contributions to their strike-bound locals, but when measured against the vast armies of strikers, these funds dwindled almost into insignificance.

J. W. Brown, J. G. Sause, Jennie Matyas and G. A. Gerber. At a meeting in Madison Square Garden on November 8 a collection of $150,000 was taken up. Many local unions, notably those of Altoona, Pa., gave half their local treasuries and assessed their members one day's pay each. The Marine Engineers, local 33 of New York, contributed $10,000; the International Fur Workers' Union $20,000; the International Ladies Garment Workers' Union, $60,000; and the Amalgamated Clothing Workers of America, $100,000. All these donations were highly praiseworthy, but especially the last one mentioned, because the organization making it is not affiliated to, nor even in good grace with, the A. F. of L.

The total amount collected and turned over to the National Committee was $418,141.14. This more than covered the entire cost of the commissariat, leaving $69,631.42 to be applied to other expenses. Thus, taking them as a whole, the cooperating international unions in the National Committee were not required to pay a penny to the feeding of the strikers and their families. The commissariat was a monument to the solidarity of Labor generally with the embattled steel workers.

Naturally, the employers bitterly hated the commissaries. They sneered at the quantity and quality of the food given out by them, and in many places printed handbills in several languages advising the strikers to go at once to union headquarters and demand strike benefits in cash. And by the same token, the strikers held the commissaries in high esteem. The foreign-born among them especially, would stand around watching with never-ceasing wonder and enthusiasm the stream of men and women coming forth laden with supplies. To them there was something sacred about the food. Many of them in desperate circumstances had to be practically compelled to accept it; not because they felt themselves objects of charity, but because they thought others needed help worse than they. They conceived the whole thing as a living demonstration of the solidarity of labor. The giving of the food produced an effect upon their morale far better than could have come from the distribution of ten times its value in money. The commissariat enormously strengthened the strikers. Without it the strike would have collapsed many weeks before it did. Unions in future great walkouts will do well to study the steel strike commissary plan.

Strikes, even the smallest, affect so many people in so many ways that it is difficult under the best of circumstances to compile accurate data upon their cost. In the case of the steel strike it is next to impossible to do so. The great number of steel companies and the armies of men involved; the wide scope of the strike; the condition of outlawry in many steel districts; the fact that the strike was lost; the workers' numerous nationalities and imperfection of organization — all these and various other factors make it exceedingly difficult, at least at this early date, to give more than a hint of the strike's cost.

In the steel strike, as in all others, the burden of suffering fell to the workers' lot. To win their cause they gave freely of their lives, liberty, blood and treasure. A poll of the National Committee local secretaries yields the following list of strike dead:

Buffalo	2
Chicago	1
Cleveland	1
Farrell	4
Hammond	4
Newcastle	2
Pittsburgh	1
West Natrona	2
Wheeling	1
Youngstown	2
Total	20

The killed were all on the strikers' side, except two. The above list properly includes Mrs. Fannie Sellins. But it does not include the scores of scabs who, because of their own or other incompetent workers' ineptness, were roasted, crushed to death, or torn to pieces in the dangerous steel-making processes during the strike. Although the steel companies were exceedingly alert in suppressing the names of these ignoble victims to their greed, it is a well-known fact that there were many of them. There was hardly a big mill anywhere that did not have several to its account.

How many hundreds of strikers were seriously injured by being clubbed and shot will never be known, because most of them, especially in Pennsylvania, healed themselves as best they might. With good grounds they feared that disclosing their injuries to doctors would lead to their arrest upon charges of rioting. The number of arrested strikers ran into the thousands. But so orderly were the strikers that few serious charges could be brought against them. They were jailed in droves and fined heavily mostly for minor " offenses." Except in Butler, Pa., where a score of strikers were arrested for stopping a car of scabs on the way to work (framed-up by the State Police) and sent to the penitentiary, no strikers anywhere in the whole strike zone received heavy jail sentences. Considering the terrific provocations offered the men and the extreme eagerness with which the courts punished them, this remarkable record is an eloquent testimonial to their orderliness.[1] Of course, the companies did not neglect to avail themselves of the heartless blacklist. Just now hundreds of their former employees, denied work and forced to break up their homes and leave town, are criss-crossing the country looking for opportunities to make new starts in life.

As for the cost to the strikers in wages, the Philadelphia *Public Ledger* of January 10, two days after the strike was called off, carried a special telegram from Pittsburgh, stating (authority not quoted) that the wage loss in that district was $48,005,060.35, specified as follows:

[1] This was largely because the men were sober. In fact, prohibition helped the steel campaign in several important respects; (1) because having no saloons to drown their troubles in, the workers, clear-headed, attended the union meetings and organized more readily; (2) when the strike came they did not waste their few pennies on liquor and then run back to work in the old way; they bought food with them and stayed on strike; (3) being sober, they were the better able to avoid useless violence and to conduct their strike effectively.

Clarksburg, W. Va.	$310,000.00
Wheeling District	6,100,000.00
Donora	1,200,000.00
Steubenville dist.	2,260,000.00
Youngstown	15,500,000.00
Monessen	2,660,000.00
Brackenridge	450,000.00
New Kensington	375,000.00
McKeesport	597,869.00
Port Vue	900,000.00
Sharon-Farrell	1,250,000.00
New Castle	705,000.00
Homestead	737,840.00
Duquesne	55,030.00
Johnstown	5,712,321.35
Ellwood City	35,000.00
Butler	1,450,000.00
Aliquippa	10,000.00
Pittsburgh	5,715,000.00
Sharpsburg, Ætna	435,000.00
Vandergrift	357,000.00
Clairton	165,000.00
Rankin	375,000.00
Braddock	650,000.00

To the above, the New York *Herald* of January 12 editorially adds an estimate of $39,000,000 for steel districts other than Pittsburgh, making a grand total of $87,000,000 as the strikers' wage loss. But these figures, bearing the earmarks of Steel Trust origin, are too low. On the basis of the minimum figures of an average of 250,000 strikers for 90 working days (actual strike length 108 days) at $5.00 per day per man, we arrive at a total of $112,500,000.00, or $450.00 per average striker.

Doubtless these figures are also too low, but they will serve to indicate the tremendous sums of money the already poverty-stricken steel workers were willing to sacrifice in order to change the conditions which Mr. Gary so glowingly paints as ideal.

The loss to the steel companies must have been enormous. Without doubt it runs into several hundred millions of dollars. The items going to make up this huge bill are many and at this time impossible of accurate estimate. There must have been not only a complete cessation of profits during the strike period, but also a vast outlay of money to finance the strike-breaking measures, such as maintaining scores of thousands of gunmen to guard the plants; paying rich graft to employment offices and detective agencies for recruiting armies of scabs, who, receiving high strike wages, idled for weeks around the plants, shooting craps, playing cards, pitching quoits, and absolutely refusing to work; keeping on the payroll great staffs of office workers with nothing to do, and high paid skilled workers doing the work of common laborers; corrupting police and court officials to give the strikers the worst of it, etc., etc. Besides, there should be added the cost of repairing the great injuries done the furnaces by their sudden shutting down, this item alone amounting to many millions of dollars. But a more important factor than all, perhaps, in counting the cost of the strike to the companies was the serious injury done to their wonderful producing organization by the permanent loss of thousands of competent men who have quitted the industry; the dislocation of many thousands more from jobs for which they were well fitted and the substitution in their places of green men; the lowering of the men's morale generally, due to disappointment and bitterness at the loss of the strike, etc. We may depend upon it that the companies, following out their policy of minimizing the strike's effects, will so juggle their financial and tonnage statements as to make it impossible for years to figure out what it really cost them, if it can ever be done.

The cost to the people at large is indicated by the New York *Sun,* quoted by the *Literary Digest,* January 31, 1920, as follows:

> There was the loss to the railroads not only in freights from the steel plants, but in freights from general mills and factories which, failing to get their steel supplies, could not maintain their production and fulfill their own deliveries. There was the loss in wages in such mills and factories due to that failure to get their material on which their wage-earners could work. There was the loss in such communities to trade folk whose customers thus had their spending power reduced by the steel strike.— Hence this loss of steel tonnage begins at once to widen until the loss eventually could be figured in the billions.

For the privilege of having an autocracy in the steel industry the American people pay not only huge costs in unearned dividends each year, but also, occasionally, such monster special charges as the above. Garyism is an expensive luxury.

The foregoing figures and statements merely serve to point out the immensity of the steel strike by indicating its approximate cost to the strikers, the steel companies, and the public. Admittedly they are but loose estimates, based upon scanty data. Absolute accuracy is not claimed for them. The expenditures of the labor movement in the campaign can be more closely calculated, although they, too, are far from definite. They fall into three general classes: (1) those by the general office of the National Committee for Organizing Iron and Steel Workers; (2) those by the A. F. of L. and co-operating international steel trades unions not through the office of the National Committee; (3) those by local steel workers' councils and unions from their own treasuries. Of these the latter may be eliminated as impossible of estimation, there being so many local organizations involved and the after-strike conditions so unfavorable to statistics gathering. They were a minor element of expense compared to the other two, which we will try to approximate as closely as may be.

1. From the beginning of the steel campaign, August 1, 1918, until January 31, 1920, the total net disbursements of the National Committee for all purposes, after making deductions for refunds, transfers, etc., amounted to $525,702.72. This stretch of time may be divided into two parts: (a) Organizing period, from August 1, 1918, until September 22, 1919 — during which time virtually all the 250,000 men enrolled in the campaign (see end of Chapter VII) had joined the unions; (b), Strike period, from September 22, 1919, until January 31, 1920 — during which time the heavy special strike expenses were incurred. This period is extended

three weeks past the date of the strike's close, because the commissariat was still in operation and other important strike expenses were going on.

The total net disbursements made by the National Committee during the organizing period were $73,139.66, which amounts to a small fraction over 29 cents for each of the 250,000 men organized. The total net disbursements of the National Committee during the strike period were $452,563.06, or $1.81 for each of the 250,000 average strikers. Adding these two figures together gives $2.10 as the cost to the National Committee of organizing each steel worker and taking care of him during the whole strike.

2. The disbursements of the National Committee covered general organizing and strike expenses, such as commissary, legal, rent, printing, salaries, etc. The A. F. of L. and the co-operating international unions also incurred heavy expenses upon their own account, whose chief items were for keeping organizers in the field, paying strike benefits, and making lump donations to strike-bound local unions. At this date these expenditures may be only approximated.

For the above bodies almost the sole expense during the organizing period was for maintaining organizers. Forty would be a fair average of the number of these men actually kept at the steel industry work. In the earlier part of the campaign the number was far less; in the later part, considerably more. The cost of maintaining them per month may be set at not more than $400.00 each, for salaries and general expenses. Thus, for the 13¾ months of the organizing period the expense to the A. F. of L. and co-operating unions for this item would be about $220,000, or 88 cents per man organized. This is a top figure.

During the strike period, on an average, 75 organizers were kept in the field by these bodies. Due to increases in wages, etc., their upkeep should be calculated at about $500.00 per month each. For 4¼ months, September 22 to January 31, our strike period, this would amount to $159,375. To this should be added $100,000, which according to reports received approximates what the organizations paid in strike benefits and donations direct to their strikers and not through the office of the National Committee. This would make their total expenditures for the strike period $259,375, or slightly less than $1.04 per striker. Adding together the amounts for the organizing period and the strike period, we arrive at a grand total of $479,375, or $1.92 per man, spent during the entire campaign by the A. F. of L. and co-operating internationals.

The figures for the A. F. of L. and co-operating internationals are estimates,— the constant shifting of organizers during the campaign, their widely varying rates of pay, etc., making accuracy impossible. But from my knowledge of what went on I will venture that the figures cited are close enough to the reality to give a fair conception of this class of expenditures.

Combining the National Committee expenditures with those of the A. F. of L. and co-operating unions, we arrive at the following totals:

ORGANIZING PERIOD:

	Expenditures	Per Man
By Nat. Com. ....$ 73,139.66		$.29
By A. F. L. & Unions.. 220,000.00		.88
Total cost of organizing work....	$293,139.66	$1.17

STRIKE PERIOD:

By Nat. Com. $452,563.06		$1.81
By A. F. L. & Unions.. 259,375.00		1.04
Total cost of strike	$711,938.06	$2.85

WHOLE CAMPAIGN:

Total cost to Nat. Com., A. F. L. & Unions	$1,005,007.72	$4.02

In order to approximate more closely the actual cost of the campaign to the A. F. of L. and the twenty-four co-operating internationals forming the National Committee, the total of $479,375, figured in a previous paragraph as their independent expenditures, must be increased by $101,047.52, the amount they contributed directly to the National Committee for organizing and for strike expenses during the course of the campaign; [1] making a grand total out-

[1] This sum represents the actual cash given by these affiliated organizations directly to the National Committee throughout the entire movement. It divides itself as follows:

Blacksmiths ....$	6,273.28
Boilermakers	10,448.92
Bricklayers	4,199.05
P. & S. Iron Workers	7,335.78
Coopers	907.76
Electrical Workers	6,138.80
Engineers	100.00
Firemen	2,395.53
Foundry Employees	1,030.51
Hod Carriers	1,350.00
Iron, Steel and Tin Workers	11,881.81
Machinists	16,622.33
Mine, Mill, Smelter Workers	3,583.53

lay for them of $580,422.52. This in turn should be reduced by $118,451.23, the amount in the National Committee treasury on January 31, 1920. Against the remaining $461,971.29 must be checked off what the steel workers paid into these organizations in initiation fees and dues.

Inasmuch as the co-operating internationals received directly $1.00 to $2.00 (mostly the latter) from the initiation fees of the approximately 250,-000 steel workers signed up during the campaign, not to speak of thousands of dollars in per capita tax from armies of dues payers over a period of many months, it is safe to say that their net outlay of $461,971.29 would be nearly if not altogether offset by their income. It is true that some of the organizations, like the Miners and the A. F. of L. itself made large expenditures, with little return; and that others, like the Structural Iron Workers, broke about even; while the Amalgamated Association put a huge sum in its treasury. All things considered, taking the twenty-four organizations as a whole, one is not much wrong in saying that so far as their national treasuries were concerned, the great movement of the steel workers, including the organizing

Mine Workers	2,600.00
Molders	4,199.05
Pattern Makers	615.52
Plumbers	2,581.04
Quarry Workers	412.50
Railway Carmen	10,448.30
Seamen	3,081.04
Switchmen	4,115.52
Sheet Metal Workers	100.00
Steam Shovelmen	627.25
Total	$101,047.52

campaign and the strike, was, financially speaking, just about self-sustaining.

Was the steel strike, then, worth the great suffering and expenditure of effort that it cost the steel workers? I say yes; even though it failed to accomplish the immediate objects it had in view. No strike is ever wholly lost. Even the least effective of them serve the most useful purpose of checking the employers' exploitation. They are a protection to the workers' standards of life. Better by far a losing fight than none at all. An unresisting working class would soon find itself on a rice diet. But the steel strike has done more than serve merely as a warning that the limit of exploitation has been reached; it has given the steel workers a confidence in their ability to organize and to fight effectively, which will eventually inspire them on to victory. This precious result alone is well worth all the hardships the strike cost them.

XIII

PAST MISTAKES AND FUTURE PROBLEMS

LABOR'S LACK OF CONFIDENCE — INADEQUATE
EFFORTS — NEED OF ALLIANCE WITH MINERS
AND RAILROADERS — RADICAL LEADERSHIP AS A
STRIKE ISSUE — MANUFACTURING REVOLUTIONS
— STRIKES: RAILROAD SHOPMEN, BOSTON POLICE,
MINERS, RAILROAD YARD AND ROAD MEN — DE-
FECTION OF AMALGAMATED ASSOCIATION

In preceding chapters I have said much about the
injustices visited upon the steel workers by the steel
companies and their minions; the mayors, burgesses,
police magistrates, gunmen, State Police, Senate
Committees, etc. But let there be no mistake. I
do not blame the failure of the strike upon these
factors. I put the responsibility upon the shoulders
of Organized Labor. Had it but stirred a little the
steel workers would have won their battle, despite
all the Steel Trust could do to prevent it.

By this I mean no harsh criticism. On the contrary, I am the first to assert that the effort put forth
in the steel campaign was wonderful, far surpassing
anything ever done in the industry before, and marking a tremendous advance in trade-union tactics.
Yet it was not enough, and it represented only a
fraction of the power the unions should and could
have thrown into the fight. The organization of

[234]

the steel industry should have been a special order of business for the whole labor movement. But unfortunately it was not. The big men of Labor could not be sufficiently awakened to its supreme importance to induce them to sit determinedly into the National Committee meetings and to give the movement the abundant moral and financial backing so essential to its success. Official pessimism, bred of thirty years of trade-union failure in the steel industry, hung like a mill-stone about the neck of the movement in all its stages.

At the very outset this pessimism and lack of faith dealt the movement a fatal blow. When the unions failed to follow the original plan of the campaign (outlined in Chapter III) to throw a large crew of organizers into the field at the beginning and thus force a settlement with the steel companies during war time, as they could easily have done, they made a monumental blunder, one for which Organized Labor will pay dearly. Notwithstanding all their best efforts in the long, bitter organizing campaign and the great strike, the organizers could not overcome its effects. It was a lost opportunity that unquestionably cost the unionization of the steel industry.

And the same pessimism which caused this original deadly mistake made itself felt all through the steel campaign, by so restricting the resources furnished the National Committee as to practically kill all chance of success. Probably no big modern trade-union organizing campaign and strike has been conducted upon such slender means. Considering the great number of men involved, the viciousness of the opposition and the long duration of the movement (18 months), the figure cited in the previous chapter as covering the general expenses, $1,005,007.72, is unusually low. It amounts to but $4.02 per man, or hardly a half week's strike benefits for each. Compared to the sums spent in other industrial struggles, it is proportionally insignificant. For example, in the great coal miners' strike in Colorado, begun September 23, 1913, and ended December 10, 1914, the United Mine Workers are authoritatively stated to have spent about $5,000,000.00 As there were on an average about 12,000 strikers, this would make the cost somewhere about $400.00 per man involved. And in those days a dollar was worth twice as much as during the steel strike. Had a fraction of such amounts been available to the steel workers they would have made incomparably a better fight.

The unions affiliated with the National Committee have at least two million members. Even if they had spent outright the total sum required to carry on the organizing campaign and strike it would not have strained them appreciably. But they did not spend it, nor any considerable part of it. In the previous chapter we have seen that with donations from the labor movement at large, and initiation fees and dues paid in by the steel workers, the movement was virtually self-sustaining as far as the co-operating unions were concerned — taking them as a whole. Now, in the next campaign, all that must be different. The unions will have to put some real money in the fight. Then they may win it.

When I say that there was a shortage of resources in the steel campaign I include particularly organizers from the respective international unions. Of these there were not half enough. Often the National Committee had to beg for weeks to have a man sent in to organize a local union, the members for which it had already enrolled. Hundreds of local unions suffered and many a one perished outright for want of attention. Whole districts had to be neglected, with serious consequences when the strike came.

Moreover, the system used by many internationals in handling their organizers was wrong. They controlled them from their several general headquarters, shifting them around or pulling them out of the work without regard to the needs of the campaign as a whole. This tended to create a loose, disjointed, undisciplined, inefficient organizing force. It was indefensible. Now, in the next drive there are two systems which might be used. (1) The international unions could definitely delegate a certain number of organizers to the campaign and put them entirely under the direction of the National Committee. This was the plan followed by the A. F. of L., the Miners, and the Railway Carmen. It worked well and tended to produce a homogeneous, well-knit, controllable, efficient organizing force. (2) The organizers definitely assigned to the steel campaign by the internationals could be formed into crews, each crew to be controlled by one man and charged with looking after the needs of its particular trade. The Mine, Mill and Smelter Workers, Machinists, and Electrical Workers used this system to some extent. A series of such crews, working vertically along craft lines while the National

Committee men worked horizontally along industrial lines, would greatly strengthen the general movement. When the strike came it would not only be an industrial strike but twenty-four intensified craft strikes as well. Of the two systems, the first is probably the better, and the second, because of the individualism of the unions, the more practical. Either of them is miles superior to the plan of controlling the field organizers from a score of headquarters knowing very little of the real needs of the situation.

But more than men and money, the steel workers in their great fight lacked practical solidarity from closely related trades. In their semi-organized condition they were unable to withstand alone the terrific power of the Steel Trust, backed by the mighty capitalistic organizations which rushed to its aid. They needed from their organized fellow workers help in the same liberal measure as Mr. Gary received from those on his side. And help adequate to the task could have come only by extending the strike beyond the confines of the steel industry proper.

When the steel unions end their present educational campaign and launch the next big drive to organize the steel workers (which should be in a year or two) they ought to be prepared to meet the formidable employer combinations sure to be arrayed against them by opposing to them still more formidable labor combinations. The twenty-four unions should by then be so allied with the miners' and railroad men's organizations that should it come to a strike these two powerful groups of unions would rally to their aid and paralyse the steel industry completely by depriving it of those essentials without which it cannot operate, fuel and rail transportation. How effective such assistance would be was well indicated by the speedy and wholesale shutting down of steel mills, first during the general strike of bituminous miners in November and December of 1919, and then during the " outlaw " railroad strike in April, 1920. With such a combination of allied steel, mine and railroad workers confronting them, there is small likelihood that the steel companies (or the public at large) would consider the question of the steel workers' right to organize of sufficient importance to fight about. Mr. Gary might then be brought to a realization that this is not Czarist Russia, and that the men in his mills must be granted their human rights.

That the miners and railroaders have sufficient interests at stake to justify their entrance into such a combination no union man of heart will attempt to deny. Not to speak of the general duty of all unionists to extend help to brothers in trouble, the above-mentioned groups have the most powerful reasons of their own to work for the organization of the steel industry. The United States Steel Corporation and so-called " independent " steel mills are the stronghold of industrial autocracy in America. Every union in the labor movement directly suffers their evil effects in lower wages, longer hours and more difficult struggles for the right to organize than they otherwise would have. No union will be safe until these mills are under the banner of Organized Labor. Beyond question the organization of the steel workers would tremendously benefit the miners and railroaders. The latter cannot possibly do too much to assist in bringing it about. It is their own fight.

For the miners and railroad men to join forces with the steel workers would mean no new departure in trade-unionism. It would be merely proceeding in harmony with the natural evolution constantly taking place in the labor movement. For instance, to go no further than the two industries in question, it is only a few years since the miners negotiated agreements and struck, district by district. Even though one section walked out, the rest would remain at work. And as for the railroaders, they followed a similar plan upon the basis of one craft or one system. Each unit of the two industries felt itself to be virtually a thing apart from all the others when it came to common action against the employers. It was the heyday of particularism, of craft unionism complete. And anyone who did not think the system represented the acme of trade-union methods was considered a crank. But both groups of organizations are fast getting away from such infantile practices. We now find the miners striking all over the country simultaneously, and the railroad men rigging up such wide-spreading combinations among themselves that soon a grievance of a section hand in San Diego, California will be the grievance of an engineer in Bangor, Maine. The man who would advocate a return to the old method of each for himself and the devil take the hindmost would be looked upon today, to say the least, with grave suspicion.

During the recent steel strike the National Committee tried to arrange a joint meeting with the officials of the miners and railroad brotherhoods to see if some assistance, moral if nothing else, could be secured for the steel workers. But nothing came of it. In the next big drive, however, these powerful organizations should be allied with the steel workers and prepared to give them active assistance if necessary. And in the tuning and timing of movements to permit of such a condition, so that no lots, legal or contractual, need be cut across, there are involved no technical problems which a little initiative and far-sightedness on the part of the labor men in control could not readily overcome.

In order to cover up their own inveterate opposition to Organized Labor in all its forms and activities, and to blind the workers to the real cause of the defeat, namely lack of sufficient power on the employees' side, great employing interests caused to be spread over the whole country the statement that the steel strike failed because of radical leadership, and that if such "dangerous" men as John Fitzpatrick and myself had not been connected with it everything would have been lovely. They were especially severe against me for my "evil" influence on the strike. But somehow their propaganda did not seem to strike root among labor men, especially those who were backing the steel campaign. The workers are getting too keen these days to let the enemy tell them who shall or shall not be their officials; and when they see one of these officials made the target of bitter attack from such notorious interests as the Steel Trust they are much inclined to

[241]

feel that he is probably giving them a square deal.

As for myself, and I know John Fitzpatrick took the same position regarding himself, I was willing to resign my position on the National Committee the very instant it was indicated by those associated with me that my presence was injuring the movement. I felt that to be my duty. But to the last, that indication never came. When I finally resigned as Secretary-Treasurer on January 31, it was entirely of my own volition.

The avalanche of vituperation and personal abuse was started several months before the strike, when a traitor labor paper in Pittsburgh (one of the stripe which lives by knifing strikes and active unionists for the employers) published articles containing quotations from the " red book," and the other stuff later bruited about in the daily press. To hear this sheet tell it, the revolution was at hand. Immediately after the articles appeared I sent copies to the presidents of all the twenty-four co-operating unions, with the result that almost all of these officials wrote me, advising that I pay no attention to these attacks, but continue with my work. They seemed to consider it something of a compliment to be so bitterly assailed from such a quarter. Again, at the very moment when President Gompers was dictating his letter to Judge Gary asking for a conference (long after the above-mentioned attacks) I stated that possibly too much prominence for me in the movement might attract needless opposition to it and I offered to resign from the conference committee which handled all negotiations concerning the steel strike. But my objections were over-ruled and

I was continued on the committee. Moreover, at any time in the campaign a word from the executive officers of the A. F. of L. would have brought about my resignation. This they were aware of for months before the strike. All of which indicates that the men responsible for the organizations in the movement were satisfied that it was being carried on according to trade-union principles, and also that in consideration of the Steel Trust's murderous tactics in the past it was a certainty that if the opposition had not taken the specific form it did, it would have manifested itself in some other way as bad or worse. It was to be depended upon that some means would have been found to thoroughly discredit the movement.

This conviction was intensified by the unexampled fury with which each important move of Labor during the past year has been opposed, not only by employers but by governmental officials as well. All through the war the moneyed interests watched with undisguised alarm and hatred the rapid advance of the unions; but they were powerless to stop it. Now, however, they are getting their revenge. The usual method of defeating such movements during this period of white terrorism is to attach some stigma to them; to question the legitimacy of their aims, and then, when the highly organized and corrupted press has turned public sentiment against them, to crush them by the most unscrupulous means. It makes no difference how mild or ordinary the movement is, some issue is always found to poison public opinion against it.

The first important body of workers to feel the

[243]

weight of this opposition was the railroad shop-men. The Railroad Administration having dilly-dallied along with their demands for several months, these under-paid workers, goaded on by the mounting cost of living, finally broke into an unauthorized strike in the early summer of 1919. This almost destroyed the organizations. Officials who ought to know declared that at one time over 200,-000 men were out. Naturally the press roundly denounced them as Bolsheviki. Upon a promise of fair treatment they returned to work. When the matter finally came to President Wilson for settlement, he declared that to raise wages would be contrary to the Government's policy of reducing the cost of living, and requested that the demands be held in abeyance. This statement was a Godsend to all the reactionary elements, who used it to break up wage movements everywhere. Thus came to grief the effort of the shopmen. Up to May, 1920, they have secured no relief whatsoever.

Next came the affair of the Boston police in September, 1919. This developed from an effort of typically conservative policemen to organize. The strike was deliberately forced by the action of State politicians, inspired by big business, in cold-bloodedly discharging a number of the officers of the new union and stubbornly refusing to re-instate them. When the inevitable strike occurred they labelled it not merely an attempted revolution, but a blow at the very foundations of civilization. The press did the rest. The strike was buried beneath a deluge of abuse, misrepresentation and vilification.

Then came the coal miners in November, 1919.

A GROUP OF ORGANIZERS

Standing, left to right: W. Searl, F. Wilson, A. V. Craig, M. Mestrovich, E. Martin, J. M. Peters, R. W. Beattie, J. Moskus, S. Coates, J. Manley, *Striker*, T. A. Harris, E. O. Gunther, B. J. Damich, *Striker*, C. Foley, M. Bellam, T. A. Daley, *Striker*, W. Z. Foster. Seated, left to right: J. Lenahan, F. J. Sweek, J. Klinsky, F. Wiernicki, I. Liberti, A. DeVerneuil, C. Claherty, J. N. Aten, J. W. Hendricks, S. Rokosz, R. W. Reilly, J. A. Norrington, F. Kurowsky, J. G. Brown, G. W. Troutman, J. E. McCadden, W. Murphy, S. T. Hammersmark.

During the war this body of men sent fully 60,000 members to the front in France. They bought untold amounts of liberty bonds and worked faithfully to keep the industries in operation. But no sooner did they make demand for some of the freedom which they thought they had won in the war than they found themselves crowded into a strike, and their conservative, old-line, trade-union leaders harshly assailed as revolutionists. For instance, said Senator Pomerene:[1]

> Years ago the American spirit was startled because a Vanderbilt had said, "The public be damned." But Vanderbilt seems to have no patent on the phrase, or if he had it is being infringed today by men who have as little regard for the public welfare as he himself had. There is no difference in kind between him and a Foster, who, aided by the extreme Socialist and I. W. W. classes of the country, aims to enlist under his leadership all the iron and steel workers of a nation and to paralyze industry, or a Lewis (President of the United Mine Workers of America), who, to further his own ambitions, aided as he was by the same elements, calls 400,000 men out of the mines and says to the public, "Freeze or starve."

The Government condemned the strike as "unjustifiable and unlawful" and invoked against it the so-called Lever law. This law, a war measure against food and fuel profiteers, was, when up for adoption, distinctly stated by its author, Representative Lever, and by Attorney General Gregory, as not applying to workers striking for better conditions.[2]

[1] Quoted from *The Coopers' Journal* for February, 1920.
[2] For important details, see article entitled "The Broken Pledge," by Samuel Gompers, in the *American Federationist*, January, 1920.

Moreover, since the armistice it had fallen into disuse,— as far as employers were concerned; but upon the strength of it the miners' strike was outlawed, Federal Judge Anderson issuing an injunction which commanded the union officials to rescind the strike order and to refuse all moral and financial assistance to the strikers. Rarely has a labor union found itself in so difficult a situation. The only thing that saved the miners from a crushing defeat was their splendid organization and strategic position in industry. On November 11, after the union officials had agreed to rescind the strike order, the Philadelphia *Public Ledger* expressed an opinion widely held when it said:

> The truth of the matter is that we all "got in wrong" on this coal situation. This is the time to say in entire frankness that *the Government handled the situation with the tact, timeliness and conciliatory spirit of a German war governor jack-booting a Belgium town into docility.*

And now we have the unauthorized strike of the Railroad yard and road men; this is clearly an outbreak of workers exasperated on the one hand by a constantly increasing cost of living, and on the other by dilatory methods of affording relief. The orthodox tactics are being employed to break it. The Lever law, disinterred from the legislative graveyard to beat the miners, has been galvanized into life again and is being used to jail the strike leaders. This is not all, however. Probably there never was a big strike in this country more spontaneous and unplanned than the one in question. But that does not worry our Department of Justice; it has just announced to a credulous world that the whole affair is a highly organized plot to overthrow the Government. Within the hour I write this (on April 15) I read in the papers that I have been singled out by Attorney-General Palmer as one of the strike leaders. Eight-column headlines flare out the charge, " PALMER BLAMES FOSTER FOR RAIL STRIKE," etc.[1]

To Mr. Palmer's " penny dreadful " plot, the local newspapers add lying details of their own. The Pittsburgh *Leader,* for instance, recites *in extenso* how I returned from the West in disguise to Pittsburgh several days ago — presumably after a trip plotting with Mr. Palmer's wonderful revolutionaries, who not only can bring whole industries to a standstill by a wave of the hand, but can do it in such a manner that although many thousands of workers are " in the know " the Department of Justice never gets to hear about it until the strikes have occurred.

Now the fact is that I have been so busy writing this book that I have hardly stirred from the house for weeks. Since the steel strike ended I have not been beyond the environs of Pittsburgh. Moreover, I do not know a solitary one of the men advertised as strike leaders, nor has there been any communication whatsoever between us. I have not attended any strike meetings, nor have I even seen a man whom I knew to be a striker. But of course such details are irrelevant to the Department of Justice and the newspapers. The latter boldly an-

1 Pittsburgh *Post,* April 15, 1920.

nounce that it is officially hoped that Mr. Palmer's charges will stampede the men back to work.[1]   In fact that is their aim.   These charges are a strike-breaking measure, pure and simple, and have no necessary relation to truth.[2]

Similar instances might be multiplied to illustrate the extreme virulence of the attacks on Labor in late struggles — how the press manufactured the general strikes in Seattle and Winnipeg into young revolutions; and how even when Mr. Gompers announced some time back that the American Federation of Labor would continue its customary political policy of " rewarding its friends and punishing its

[1] Pittsburgh *Chronicle-Telegraph*, April 15, 1920.

[2] In connection with this matter I promptly called Mr. Palmer a liar, a statement which was widely carried by the press. Our would-be tyrant swallowed it. In the situation two courses were open to him: If his accusations against me were true, under his own interpretation of the Lever law he was duty-bound to arrest me; and if they were not true, common justice demanded that he admit the incorrectness of the statements he had sent flying through the press, attacking me. But he has done neither. And in the meantime I have been subjected to a storm of journalistic abuse. For example, says the Donora, Pa. *Herald* of April 16: "Wm. Z. Foster seems determined to have that little revolution if he has to get out and start one himself. About the best remedy for that bird would be one of those oldfashioned hangings."

One can readily imagine how quickly the wheels of justice would have whirled and how speedily the editor would have been clapped into jail were such an incitement to murder printed in a labor journal. But when the case in point was called to the attention of the Pittsburgh officials of the Department of Justice they could do nothing about it. Nor could those of the Post Office Department, although the Donora *Herald* circulates through the mails. Similarly the county and state officials could see no cause for action. Finally the opportunities for relief sifted down to a libel suit. And what chance has a workingman in such a suit against a henchman of the Steel Trust in the heart of Pennsylvania's black steel district?

enemies," the scheme was denounced in influential quarters as an attempt to capture the Government and set up a ·dictatorship of the proletariat. But enough. The steel strike was a drive straight at the heart of industrial autocracy in America; it could expect to meet with nothing less than the most desperate and unscrupulous resistance. If the issue used against the strike had not been the charge of radical leadership, we may rest assured there would have been another " just as good." The next movement will have to win by its own strength, rather than by the vagaries of a newspaper-created public opinion.

But a far more pressing problem even than any of those touched upon in the foregoing paragraphs is the one involved in the attitude of the Amalgamated Association of Iron, Steel and Tin Workers toward the steel campaign. This organization withdrew from the National Committee immediately after the strike was called off, and it has apparently abandoned trying, at least for the time being, to organize the big steel mills. Thus the whole campaign is brought to the brink of ruin, because the Amalgamated Association has jurisdiction over about 50 per cent. of the workers in the mills, including all the strategic steel-making trades, without whose support the remainder cannot possibly win. Unless it can be brought back to the fold, the joint movement of the trades in the steel industry will almost certainly be broken up, to the great glee of Mr. Gary and his associates.

This action was in logical sequence to the position taken through the campaign by several of the Amalgamated Association's general officers. From the beginning, they considered the movement with pessimism, often with hostility. It received scant cooperation from them. As related in Chapter VI, they tried to get a settlement with the U. S. Steel Corporation right in the teeth of the general movement; and their financial support was meager, to say the least.[1] For a few weeks during the strike movement, when victory seemed near, they displayed some slight enthusiasm; but this soon wore off and they adopted a policy of " saving what they could." They were exceedingly anxious to call off the strike many weeks before its close, and went about the country discouraging the men and advising them to return to work. And even worse, they attempted to make separate settlements with the steel companies. The following proposed agreement, presented to (and refused by) the Bethlehem Steel Corporation at Sparrows' Point when the strike was not yet two months old, tells its own story:

[1] In the report included at the end of Chapter VI, the Amalgamated Association is shown to have enrolled 70,026 members during the campaign. But, for the reasons cited, the figure is far too low. President Tighe gave a better idea of the number when, testifying before the Senate Committee, he said (Hearings, page 353) that the secretary had told him " that he had already issued in the neighborhood of 150,000 dues cards," and could not get them printed fast enough. For each man of this army of members, the national headquarters of the Amalgamated Association received two dollars. Yet in return the officials in charge, throughout the entire movement, gave the National Committee directly only $11,881.81 to work with. Of this, $3,881.81 was for organizing expenses, and $8,000.00 was to feed and furnish legal help to the great multitudes of strikers, half of whom were members of the Amalgamated Association. What strike help was extended in other directions was correspondingly scanty. The balance of the funds taken in is still in its treasury.

November 19th, 1919.

Agreement entered into between the Bethlehem Steel Company of Sparrows' Point, Maryland, and its employees, governing wages and conditions in the Sheet and Tin mills, and Tin House Department.

1. It is agreed that the wages and conditions agreed upon between the Western Sheet and Tin Plate Manufacturers' Association and the Amalgamated Association of Iron, Steel and Tin Workers, as agreed upon in the Atlantic City Conference, June, 1919, will be the prices and conditions paid to the employees in the above-mentioned departments.

2. That the company will also agree to the re-instatement of all their former employees, such as seek employment without any discrimination.

3. The above Agreement to expire June 30th, 1920.

During the strike the general officers of the Amalgamated Association never tired of telling how sacred they considered their contracts with the employers, and did not hesitate to jeopardize the strike by living up to them most strictly. But when it came to their obligations to the other trades it was a different story. They well knew, when they tried to make separate settlements with the U. S. Steel and Bethlehem Companies, that they were violating solemn agreements which they had entered into with the other trades in the industry, not to speak of fundamental principles of labor solidarity.

The national officials in question looked with undisguised jealousy upon the growth to importance of other unions in the industry where their own organization had operated alone so long. They lost no love on the National Committee. In fact more than one of their number seemed to take particular delight

[251]

in placing obstructions in its way. If they wanted to see the steel industry organized they certainly showed it in a peculiar manner. A goodly share of my time — not to speak of that of others — was spent plugging the holes which they punched through the dike. And apparently they always had the hearty support of their fellow officers. It is only fair to say, however, that the lesser officials and the rank and file of the Amalgamated Association strongly favored the National Committee movement and gave it their loyal cooperation.

As a justification for the Amalgamated Association officials' action in quitting the joint campaign, word is being sent through the steel industry that henceforth that organization will insist upon its broad jurisdictional claims and become an industrial union in fact, taking into its ranks and protecting workers of all classes in the steel industry. But no one familiar with the Amalgamated Association will take this seriously. It is a dyed-in-the-wool skilled workers' union, and has been such ever since its foundation forty-five years ago. Its specialty is the "tonnage men," or skilled iron and steel making and rolling trades proper. All its customs, policies and instincts are inspired by the interests of this industrial group. It has never looked after the welfare of the mechanical trades and the common laborers, even though for the past few years it has claimed jurisdiction over them. In its union mills it is the regular thing to find only the tonnage men covered by the agreements, no efforts whatever being made to take care of the other workers. It is true that during the recent campaign, due to the stimulus of the National Committee, laborers were taken in; but of the way they were handled, probably the less said the better. The incidents related in Chapter X are typical.

That the men now at the head of the Amalgamated Association will upset these craft practices and revolutionize their organization into a bona fide, vigorous industrial union is incredible to those who have seen them in action. But even if the miracle happened, even if they got rid of their mid-nineteenth century ideas and methods, adopted modern principles and systems, and put on the sweeping campaign necessary to organize the industry, it would not solve the problem. The other unions in the steel industry are not prepared to yield their trade claims to the Amalgamated Association, and any serious attempt by that organization to infringe upon them would result in a jurisdictional quarrel, so destructive as to wreck all hope of organizing the industry for an indefinite period. The unions would be so busy fighting among themselves that they would have no time, energy or ambition to fight the Steel Trust.

Progress and organization in the steel industry are to be achieved not by splitting the ranks and dividing the forces, but by consolidating and extending them. The only rational hope in the situation lies in a firm federation of all the trades in the industry, allied with the miners and railroad men in such fashion that they will extend help in case of trouble. The steel workers are fast recovering from their defeat. The educational campaign is getting results, and the work should be made a permanent institution until the industry is organized. For the Amalgamated Association to desert the field now is suicidal. It is worse; it is a crime against the labor movement. It will break up the campaign and throw the steel workers, helpless, upon the mercy of Gary and his fellow exploiters. Organized Labor should not permit it. The time is past when a few short-sighted union officials can block the organization of a great industry.

XIV

IN CONCLUSION

THE POINT OF VIEW — ARE THE TRADE UNIONS REV-
OLUTIONARY — CAMOUFLAGE IN SOCIAL WARS —
RUINOUS DUAL UNIONISM — RADICALS SHOULD
STRENGTHEN TRADE UNIONS — THE ENGLISH
RENAISSANCE — TOM MANN'S WORK

FOR those progressives who will look upon the steel
campaign from an evolutionary standpoint — that is
by a comparison with past experiences — it will stand
out in its true light as marking a great advance in
trade-union methods and practices. It is true that
the unions in the campaign made many mistakes,
quarreled seriously among themselves, and put forth
only a fraction of their real strength; but when one
considers that they substituted a group of twenty-four
unions for individual action in other campaigns;
established a standard initiation fee instead of the
multitude that existed before; adopted modern
methods of organizing in place of the antiquated system previously prevailing; organized a joint commissariat, carried on a successful organizing campaign and waged a great strike together, one must
admit that a tremendous stride forward has been
made. The conclusion is bound to be optimistic and
full of enthusiasm for the future.

But unfortunately there are large bodies of progressives who do not judge from the evolutionary viewpoint when it comes to trade unionism. These range all the way from the mildest liberals and friends of Labor to the most extreme I. W. W.'s. They form an influential group. Theirs is the idealistic method; more or less clearly, these elements hold in their mind's eye a smooth-running, intelligent, imaginary " one big union." This they use as an inelastic criterion by which to judge the trade unions. And the natural result is that, even in such cases as the steel campaign, the unions cut a sorry figure. Their weaknesses are unduly emphasized; their progressive innovations lose their import and seem but make-shift imitations of the real thing. The conclusions are necessarily pessimistic. The true significance of the epoch-making movement is lost. This viewpoint is so general and its consequences so far-reaching and detrimental, not only to the steel unions but to the whole labor movement, that perhaps a discussion of it may not be amiss at this point.

For many years radicals in this country have almost universally maintained that the trade unions are fundamentally non-revolutionary; that they have no real quarrel with capitalism, but are seeking merely to modify its harshness through a policy of mild reform. They have been pictured as lacking both the intelligence to want industrial freedom and the courage to demand it. And so often have these ideas been repeated, so slight has been the inquiry into their soundness, that they have come to be accepted in a large degree by virtually the entire left wing

[256]

of the labor movement. To these ideas, more than anything else, is due the current idealistic labor pessimism, the unsympathetic attitude toward, and general lack of understanding of, the trade unions.

Yet their falsity is readily apparent when one takes into consideration the real situation. It is an indisputable fact that the trade unions always act upon the policy of taking all they can get from their exploiters. They even overreach themselves sometimes, as a thousand lost strikes eloquently testify. Their program is directly anti-capitalistic. But let me quote from a booklet, written by myself several years ago, entitled, "Trade Unionism; The Road To Freedom," page 18:

> It is idle to say that the trade unions will rest content with anything short of actual emancipation. For they are as insatiable as the veriest so-called revolutionary unions. In the measure that their strength increases, so do their demands. They have sent wages up: 2, 3, 4, 5, 6, 7, 8 dollars per day, and hours down: 12, 11, 10, 9, 8, 7, 6, per day with all kinds of other concessions sandwiched in between. And now they are more radical in their demands than ever before in their history. Permanently satisfied trade unions under capitalism would be the eighth wonder of the world, outrivalling in interest the famous hanging gardens of Babylon. They would be impossible. With its growing power, Organized Labor will go on winning greater and greater concessions, regardless of how profound they may be. It is purest assumption to state that the trade unions would balk at ending the wages system.

So far as the tendency of their demands is concerned, there can be no question about that to anyone who will look at them squarely; the trade unions may be depended upon always to check exploitation through the wages system as far as their power enables them. The big question is whether or not they will be able to develop enough power to stop this exploitation altogether. As for me, I am confident that they will. In every country they are constantly adding to and solidifying their ranks; building ever more gigantic and militant combinations and throwing them athwart the exploiter's path. It is safe to say that if they cannot finally stop him it will be because it does not lie within the realms of possibility for the working class to produce a sufficiently powerful organization.

Why, then, have these strongly anti-capitalistic qualities been so long and generally ignored and the trade unions considered merely as palliative bodies? In my opinion it is because they, like various other aggressive social movements, have more or less instinctively surrounded themselves with a sort of camouflage or protective coloring, designed to disguise the movement and thus to pacify and disarm the opposition. This is the function of such expressions as, " A fair day's pay for a fair day's work," " The interests of Capital and Labor are identical," etc. In actual practice little or no attention is paid to them. They are for foreign consumption. The fact that those who utter them may actually believe what they say does not change the situation a particle. Most movements are blind to their own goals anyway. The important thing is the real trend of the movement, which is indisputably as I have stated above, on the one hand constantly expanding organ-

[258]

ization, and on the other constantly increasing demands. The trade unions will not *become* anticapitalistic through the conversion of their members to a certain point of view or by the adoption of certain preambles; they *are* that by their very makeup and methods. The most that can be done is to clarify their aims and intensify their efforts towards freedom.

If the trade unions instinctively throw dust in the eyes of their enemies, they do it for an altogether worthy purpose, the elevation of the standard of well-being for the mass of the people. In the case of the capitalist class we see the same principle applied to an utterly vicious end. The whole trend of the great employing interests is to set up an oligarchy of wealthy parasites, neither toiling nor spinning, yet for whom the whole body of workers would be compelled to labor in degradation and poverty. And if unopposed, they would not only bring about this condition, but in so doing would rob the people of every right they have — free speech, free press, free assemblage, legislative representation, trial by jury, and all the rest. But do they openly avow their purpose? Most assuredly not, for they know that powerful though they are they would be swept away by a wave of popular opposition. Therefore, through their newspapers and innumerable other propaganda agencies, they proceed to cover up their nefarious schemes of exploitation and oppression with hypocritical cloaks of patriotism, religion, benevolence, and the like. Their practice is one thing, their preaching something entirely different. Thus we have Garys and Rockefellers actually enslaving their workers by the most brutal methods and at the same time seeking to convince the public that what they are trying to do is to protect these workers from union domination, to preserve to them their sacred right to work for whomever they please, etc. Men such as these are knifing America and doing it in the name of 100 per cent. Americanism. They are social camouflagers par excellence.

The question may be pertinently asked, why, if camouflage is such a potent weapon in social as well as military warfare, should the true nature and tendency of the trade unions be pointed out, thus stripping the movement of its philosophic protection and leaving it bare before its enemies? The answer is that the camouflage works both ways; it deceives friends as well as enemies. It has thus to a great extent cost the unions the support of the whole left wing of the labor movement. Its advantages are outweighed by its disadvantages.

In what I have called the left wing of the movement there are large and ever-increasing numbers of workers and sympathizers who refuse to face the prospect of a society forever based upon tre wage system. They demand an organization that is making for its abolition and the substitution therefor of a system of industrial justice. If they were to look sharply, they would see that the trade-union movement is traveling faster than any other body toward the end they wish to reach. But unfortunately, looking sharply is not their method. They habitually attach too much importance to surface indications and not enough to real results. They go almost entirely by preambles and manifestoes. Consequently, taking the trade-union slogans at their face value and finding them altogether unsatisfactory, they turn their backs upon the trade-union movement and give support to the organizations which have the sort they want, the I. W. W., the W. I. I. U., etc.

This belief, that the trade unions are inherently conservative bodies, is the basis of the strong conviction that they are hopeless and that they must be supplanted by a new organization, aiming to abolish the wage system. The conception is found in some degree or other among virtually all radicals. And it has done incalculable harm to the unions. It has cost them the support of thousands of militants, of the best and most intelligent that the working class produces. These might have done a wonderful work; but their time and energies have been worse than wasted in trying to build up organizations such as the I. W. W. When one considers that the life of nearly every labor union depends upon the activities of a very small fraction of its membership, it is clear that this constant drain upon its best blood must have seriously hindered the advance of the trade-union movement. Many have complained at the slow progress it has made; but the marvel is rather that it has been able to progress at all.

This devitalizing drain must be stopped, and the great body of progressives and radicals won over to a whole-hearted support of the trade unions. I consider this one of the most important tasks confronting the labor movement. But it can be accomplished only by driving home to these elements the patent facts that the trade unions are making straight for the abolition of capitalism and that they are going incomparably faster towards this goal than any of the much advertized, so-called revolutionary unions, in spite of the latter's glittering preambles. They must be taught that the weaknesses of the trade unions are but the weaknesses of the working class, and that as the latter gradually improves in education and experience, the unions will correspondingly take on higher forms and clearer aims. You cannot have perfect organizations with imperfect workers to build upon. In a word, the progressives must be won over from the idealistic and utopian to the evolutionary point of view.

Indeed, it must be granted that insistence upon the real goal and tendency of trade unionism will provoke the capitalist class into greater opposition against the movement. But this will be trebly offset by the added support which the unions will get from the large numbers of militants who now stand apart from them because of lack of understanding. The power of even a few such men, proceeding intelligently along practical lines, is one of the marvels of the labor movement. It may be confidently expected, therefore, that when the many thousands of these, now indifferent or hostile, begin to work together, setting up their own press and systematically furthering amalgamation and federation projects to bring the unions into closer cooperation, initiating and prosecuting organizing campaigns, retiring to private life such officials as now find themselves at the head of the Amalgamated Association, etc., vast changes for the better are bound to occur in the labor movement.

The trade unions have cost the workers untold efforts to build, and in the main they seem loath to give them up, despite the blandishments of utopian dual unions. Apparently, it is through the old unions that the workers will eventually achieve their industrial freedom, save, perhaps, in such cases as the United Garment Workers, where conditions in the organization were so utterly hopeless that there was nothing to do but form a new body, the Amalgamated Clothing Workers. But this was an exceptional case. Most of the unions are moving steadily onward and upward, and they have an unshakable grip upon the workers in their respective spheres. This being so, the logical thing to do is systematically to set about improving and strengthening them. If this is done, then, instead of the wild, desperate, dualistic outbreaks and strikes, which have characterized the American labor movement for years, and done it incalculable harm, the discontented rank and file will find relief through an orderly and rapid progress within the folds of the organizations they already have. The sooner these facts are recognized the better for American Labor.

During the past few years much has been said about the wonderful progress being made by the English trade-union movement. This, I venture to assert, is due largely, if not altogether, to the absence among the radicals of England of the idealistic, dualistic attitude towards the unions which exists so widely here, and which has produced the

I. W. W. and its great body of sympathizers.
The English radicals have a better conception
than ours of the trade unions; for, flesh and blood of
the labor movement, they pit their policies and energies against the conservatives, and win. They are
the ones who are writing the highly-praised pro-
grams, and driving onward the great wage movements. They are practical and constructive. Un-
like so many of our radicals they do not waste their
time and strength in empty, pessimistic criticism of
the trade unions, and in vain, foolhardy attempts
to tear the whole labor structure to pieces and to
reconstruct it according to the dream of Daniel De
Leon.

In England the turning point came ten years ago
when she felt the great wave of sentiment for
revolutionary unionism then sweeping the world.
The question was whether this movement should
realize its aims through the old unions or by starting
new ones. The existing unions were notoriously
conservative. Several of our leading radicals had
said they were even more hopeless than our own organizations and strongly urged the formation of an
English I. W. W. But fortunately, Tom Mann and
his colleagues, with a deeper knowledge of trade
unionism, were able to forestall this movement and
to direct the strong stream of progressive thought
and energy into the old unions. The result was
magical. Within two years the great and successful
strikes of the transport workers, railroaders and
miners had occurred, and the renaissance of the English labor movement was assured. British workingmen will never realize the invaluable service which

Tom Mann rendered them in saving England from an I. W. W. dual movement, with its tremendous waste of power and its weakening effect upon the trade unions.

How long are American progressives going to continue deceiving themselves with the words of high-sounding preambles? When are they going to quit chasing rainbows and settle down to real work? These are important considerations indeed. The hour when our militants generally adopt English methods, and turn their whole-hearted attention to building up and developing the trade-union movement,— that hour will be the dawn of a new day for American Labor.

THE END

DATE DUE

GAYLORD   INTED IN U.S.A